D1163782

Motor caravanning: A Complete Guide

Motor Caravanning: A Complete Guide

Henry Myhill

Including two chapters by John Hunt,
Editor of *Motor Caravan + Camping*

A Hyperion Book
WARD LOCK LIMITED · LONDON

Acknowledgments

This book could never have been published without the generous co-operation of John Hunt. This is obvious, for he has written two of the most important chapters (including the literally vital one). But he has done far more, placing at my disposal his unrivalled experience during sixteen years as the first Editor of *The Motor Caravanner*, and as the founder-Editor of *Motor Caravan + Camping*, and answering hosts of queries from my publisher's dedicated editor during my own long absences abroad. In a wider sense, anyone who has followed the growth of motor caravanning largely through John Hunt's editorials, reports, and tests, as I like many others have done, will always approach the subject with the eyes of *Nomad* (as he sometimes signs himself). And in thanking John Hunt it goes without saying that I am thanking also Audrey, his partner not only in marriage and in journalism, but in motor caravanning.

The publishers would like to thank the manufacturers and the following individuals who supplied illustrations for use in the book: B. Barr, E. Emrys Jones, Derek Haselwood, A. Lingen-Watson, G. H. Turner and K. H. Varty.

ISBN 0 7063 5086 3

A Hyperion Book
First published in Great Britain
1976 by Ward Lock Limited,
116 Baker Street, London, W1M 2BB

House editor Sue Unstead
Designed by Andrew Shoolbred
Layout by Jill Leman

Text filmset by
Servis Filmsetting Limited,
Manchester
Printed and bound by
Editorial Fher S.A., Bilbao, Spain

Contents

Introduction

Motor caravans did not appear in any numbers on British roads until 1960, and the decade and a half of development which followed, though marked by rapid change and much innovation, has been even more remarkable for the recurrent pattern of certain themes.

The emergence of this underlying pattern, making it likely that the motor caravans of the future, however exciting, will have certain family resemblances to the motor caravans of today, means that it is now possible to write a guide to the subject which will not be out of date before it has even gone into print. Such a guide has also become possible because during those fifteen or so years the industry as a whole, and the enthusiastic consumers of its products, have created a wealth of experience, which I have tried to condense into this book.

A guide to motor caravanning is now therefore possible and probably overdue. Proof of this lies in the success of the motor caravanning press. In a publishing climate where well-established trade papers and specialist journals of all kinds have been folding up, the magazines devoted to motor caravans have gone from strength to strength. The public clearly wants to read about them. One of the first steps taken by many intending motor caravanners is to subscribe to one of these magazines, so that they can learn more before actually acquiring a vehicle.

But the magazines are not written specifically for the beginner. Over a couple of years one issue or another will probably answer most of the questions that he is likely to ask, but by the very nature of the medium these answers are not assembled in a readily accessible form. A guide is required which both satisfies his initial curiosity and goes beyond the excellent, but simple, brochures prepared by two enterprizing organizations.

Although this guide hopes to provide answers to those questions, some of which may not yet have occurred to the person contemplating his first purchase, it has not been written in question and answer form. Where tables or lists are helpful, they are given. But my aim has been to write a readable as well as a helpful book, and one which can serve veterans as well as the recently converted. If, while enjoying a cup of tea or a glass of wine in a fellow motor caravanner's vehicle, I occasionally catch sight of it on the book shelf, I shall know that I have succeeded.

1 Why a motor caravan?

The first part of this book is designed to help the reader in choosing a motor caravan. It describes the different types of model on the market, and then goes on to examine them in detail, discussing which might suit him best. Finally, at the end of the book there is a list – as complete and up-to-date as possible – of those models which are currently available.

If none of these quite matches his own requirements, or if he is a do-it-yourself enthusiast, he may prefer to undertake his own conversion. As I am not qualified to write about this myself, I have secured the co-operation of John Hunt, perhaps the best-known and certainly the most experienced writer in this particular field, who has contributed a chapter on the subject.

Many prefer to buy a second-hand van. Eventually, in any case, the time comes for a van to be sold. So the market for them is discussed, from the point of view of the seller as well as the buyer. Finally, since no motor caravan can be bought and driven away without formality, something is said about insurance.

All this is preliminary to the serious business of what you do with a van when you have got it, and later sections of the book are devoted to living and touring in your van. But before all this comes the question: why a motor caravan in the first place?

For it is not the only way of living while travelling. More people own trailer caravans than motor caravans. Others own tents, or stay in hotels. Some of these have considered purchasing a motor caravan, and have deliberately decided against it. Their reasons may help us to make up our minds as to whether we really do want one ourselves; and if so, just what we want it for.

Those who prefer trailer caravans generally do so for the greater amount of space, and for the versatility of the car-trailer combination. The caravan can be left on a site, automatically reserving a place there, while its owners can circulate in their car without having to pack everything up before driving off. If the car needs repair, the caravan is still available to provide accommodation. And when the car needs changing, the caravan remains, complete with all those personal touches and improvements which are lost when a motor caravan is sold.

All these arguments might also be used by tent campers, some of whom own veritable canvas bungalows, divided into verandahs, halls, dining rooms, kitchens, larders, built-in wardrobes, and bedrooms. Those who do not admit expense as the main reason for their choice express their preference for being closer to nature, for the open-air life.

It is generally the woman of the family who voices the reasons for staying in hotels. When she goes away she wants a holiday – a holiday, in short, from shopping, from cooking, and from washing-up.

All three categories would further argue against the motor caravan's expense: a four-figure sum of capital tied up in an asset which many would only use on holiday and occasional weekends, and which they would buy as a supplement to, instead of as a substitute for, the family car. 'You could hardly drive all that to work or shopping', they remark.

Some of the reasons given are valid enough. Motor caravans are not for everybody, but in any case, the motor caravanner has his own answers to counter every one of the above arguments.

For although most trailer vans are roomier inside, this extra space is actually less useful. The walls, which are flimsier, must not be overloaded, and when towing, the balance of the van can be upset even by placing a container full of water at the wrong end. The trailer caravan is more versatile on a site, but this must be contrasted with the greater strain on the driver and his car in getting them there. The motor caravan's rugged commercial engine, with its low-compression ratio, is likely to give less mechanical trouble than a highly-tuned car, and to require less frequent repairs or 'trade-ins'.

The motor caravanner can get closer to nature than all but the most foolhardy or illicit camper. For he can park in quiet laybys, on windy downs, or beside forest-clad lakes, where a tent would be tempting providence, if not actually forbidden.

As for hotels, the motor caravanner can take his choice when he wants a good dinner out, drinking without having to worry about the breathalyser, in the knowledge that his bed (with permission, of course) awaits him a few yards away in the hotel carpark. His wife can then dress for dinner if she wishes, and they will probably enjoy their evening and their meal much more than if they were actually staying in a hotel, having to pay for – and eat – two or more big meals each day. And even if they will not have stayed at the *Bristol*, they will have eaten at the *Grand*, the *Majestic*, the *Palace*, and the *Carlton*, besides the *Cheval Blanc* and Madame-Dupont's-at-that-little-village-near-Cahors-which-was-better-than-any-of-them. . . . There you already have one answer to the argument based on expense, and there are others.

The smaller fixed- and elevating-roof motor caravans cost only a little more than saloon cars of equivalent horsepower. Home conversions cost even less. There is not the further expense of a trailer caravan to be purchased, with all the tedium and cost of fitting a tow bar and wiring connections. And although the present price of coachbuilt, 'high-top' motor caravans seems astronomical to those of us who remember them selling at three figures, they should be compared with those of the 'clubman' type of luxury caravan, and of the powerful car which is necessary to tow it.

It is true that the larger motor caravan has a fairly heavy consumption of petrol, but this is certainly no greater than that of a powerful car when towing, while the consumption of the smaller variety is less than even the smallest car-trailer outfit. (I am comparing the Fiat 903 cc, which averages 38 mpg, with the Mini 850 cc, with which I once towed the tiniest caravan on the market, eight feet by five, and got only 35 mpg.)

However, in petrol consumption all motor caravans have one big advantage over other vehicles. It is an advantage which only gradually becomes apparent to those who use them over any length of time. They cover less miles. Hence they use not only less petrol, but less oil and less tyres, and they wear out their engines less quickly. Their mileage is lower because they need make no 'return' journeys. Where the ordinary motorist must get back home or to the hotel after his picnic, his excursion, or his business deal, the motor caravanner simply stays where he is. In other words, instead of going from A to B, and then having to return to base at A, he travels, complete with base, from A to B, stops at B overnight, and then proceeds onwards to C on the morrow.

In theory the trailer caravanner should benefit equally from this advantage. In fact, however, his mileage is increased by his need to leave his direct route to find a site. And once parked, it is the caravan which becomes his base A, to which he returns after visits to B and C.

Unlike the trailer van, a motor caravan chassis can support more rigid walls, and its weight is more widely distributed. This is because it is basically a commercial van, designed for carrying loads. Its capacious cupboards and floor-level lockers beneath the beds can be filled with whatever supplies can be bought cheaply before setting out, or *en route*. As I write these lines in my own van, somewhere in France, I have on board tea, powdered coffee, butter and tinned meat from England; wine, brandy, honey and sardines from Spain; Finnish processed cheese and Spanish ham from tax-free Ceuta; and dried figs, dates and spices from Morocco. From France I always bring tins of chestnut cream, and jam made from the blackberries which I pick whenever I spend an autumn in Brittany.

That list, of course, refers only to food. My clothes cupboard includes ski-pants hand-made in Austria for £10; a blazer tailored in Spain for half what it would have cost off-the-peg from a British chain store; corduroy trousers acquired in a Danish sale at 60p; a supply of the most comfortable and durable rubber sandals I have ever found, which retail in Morocco at 30p; and my most-envied shirt which cost me all of 75p in Andorra. Need I go on?

The greatest benefit of a motor caravan in terms of cost is naturally the ability to dispense with hotels and restaurants. The motor caravanner can do this over a longer period and with much greater comfort than the tent camper, and with less expense than the trailer caravanner. For unlike the first he can use his van all winter, and unlike the second he is not restricted to caravan sites. The veteran motor caravanner will recall long spring or autumn holidays, when no sites were open, but when for days or weeks on end he relaxed beside deserted beaches, or beneath the walls of ancient churches or châteaux – holidays which cost him no more than his food and his petrol.

As for the petrol – or its equivalent in air, sea or rail tickets – he would have had to pay for this anyway. No wonder many long-term motor caravanners, setting off yet again for the Mediterranean, or beyond, before the winter has set in, make the excuse: 'It is so much cheaper than staying at home'.

For this is just an excuse. The true motivation of the motor caravanner lies deeper. He has discovered not only a more exciting means of travelling and a cheaper form of holiday, but a way of life. When he steps into his motor caravan, not only do his horizons widen, but he shakes off most of the problems and restrictions of daily life.

Moreover he becomes, in his motor caravan, a member of another and a far wider society. This is formed in the first place by the combination of all the smaller societies in which he finds himself. Whether he stops in a Scottish village, or an Italian suburb, on a French canal bank, or a North African beach, he becomes at once a temporary part of the landscape and a temporary member of the community. For the motor caravanner establishes a more intimate relationship with the countryside than the passing motorist can ever do, and a more friendly relationship with the local population than the trailer caravanner, confined to his site, is ever allowed.

His wider society is formed, in the second place, by his fellow caravanners. They are not only of every class, but of every nationality: French and German, Dutch and Italian. Of every continent, too: Americans and Australians, Canadians and South Africans. The motor caravanner not only gets to know his own self better, but his neighbour too.

These intangible benefits are hard to set down in black and white; but I hope that something of them will be conveyed incidentally as we examine various aspects of motor caravanning.

2 Choosing a motor caravan

There are basically four types of motor caravan. Anyone setting out to choose his first van must have a clear idea of what these are.

1) The first are fixed-roof models. These are commercial vans converted as they stand. Windows are generally let into the sides, and air vents into the roof. Occasionally, where a side

A fixed-roof model. This Ford Transit with its generous interior dimensions has retained its original shape and roof after conversion by Danbury.

door also exists, the back doors are replaced by a plain wall, with a wide panoramic window. But the exterior shape and size remains the same as the original van.

2) The second are models with elevating roofs. These carry the same modifications as the previous group, but in addition the whole or part of the roof is replaced, and can be raised to provide standing room – and, incidentally, space for the provision of

An elevating-roof model. The roof is shown in its raised position on this conversion of the BLMC Sherpa by Auto-Sleepers.

upper bunks. The difference this makes to the contour when travelling is only slight, although it can be sufficient to push the height from just below to just above 6 ft 6 in, beyond which certain shipping lines impose a height surcharge. The mini-motor caravans converted from light vans and estate cars also belong almost invariably to Group 2.

3) The third are high-top models. Here the original, almost flat

A high-top model. Although the bodywork of this Volkswagen has not been changed, the substitution of a domed roof has given its owner permanent standing room.

roof has been replaced by a dome, to give permanent standing room. Sometimes this has been done deliberately for conversion to a motor caravan; in other cases it has already been fitted to a second-hand van for commercial reasons (for example, to transport long dresses). Occasionally motor manufacturers themselves offer a high-top version.

4) The fourth group are coachbuilt models. Here a complete living unit has been built on to the back of the chassis/cab or pick-up version of a van. Whether this is permanently attached,

A coachbuilt model. The cab of this Ford Transit is the only part of the exterior identical with the vehicle shown on page 12. The rest has been replaced with a wider and higher living unit extending in a luton over the cab. This Landliner was manufactured by CI Autohomes.

as in most British models, or whether it is removable, as in the American 'campers' or the recent British 'piggy-back' vans, it cannot possibly be mistaken for a commercial van. It is clearly meant to be lived in. It is also generally of larger dimensions than the bodywork it has replaced.

From what has been said it is obvious that Group 1 vans are the cheapest, but also the most manoeuvrable; while Group 4 are the most expensive and the most comfortable, but also the heaviest to handle. Groups 2 and 3 fall in a price range between these two extremes; and all things being equal (which in motor caravans they rarely are), there is little to choose between them in cost. In comfort the high-top is slightly ahead: on the other hand the elevating-roof model is a little more manoeuvrable.

The potential purchaser, therefore, already has three factors to keep in mind: comfort, manoeuvrability, and price. All three require fuller explanation.

Comfort is really another word for space. Once there is sufficient room, any accessories which make life more agreeable can be fitted. It might appear at first sight that a full-length elevating roof offers as much space as a high-top, or a coach-built model. But the extra space provided by the raised roof only comes into existence on site. In many respects, therefore, it is wasted space. It can take no roof cupboards, no full-length wardrobes, no bookshelves. It does not provide that admirable 'luton' area above the cab, which serves almost as an attic, and in some recent coachbuilt models even takes a double bed. What it does do, of course, is to prevent bumped heads – provided it is full-length – and that lumbago-like cramp which is the result of being forced to stoop over every common task.

It may also let in draughts. Few elevating roofs are completely airtight, and their thin materials – glass fibre, Plastolene, or marine ply – offer little insulation. They can make a van draughty in the winter and stuffy in the summer. The remedy of closing it removes the point of ever having it in the first place.

Width and length are also important dimensions in promoting comfort. A van which is 6 ft wide can take a transverse bed. This will avoid exposure of the sleeper's body to an outside wall, and to the chills and rheumatism which such exposure can induce on a night of bitter wind. It will also provide more wall space for other fixtures, with less space being taken up by the beds down the length of the van. Every foot of extra length, equally, seems to add a new dimension to the vehicle.

But of course all this extra room decreases manoeuvrability. What distinguishes a motor caravan from a trailer or a tent is its 'get-up-and-go' quality. Anything which makes it more cumbersome detracts from this. When the impedimenta which go to make up comfort become a very literal burden, making it an effort to U-turn, difficult to park, a strain to drive a normal day's motoring distance, then the van's size is above that 'optimum', which must always vary with each individual.

Even storage space can be overdone. In a van, as in a house, belongings tend to expand to take up the available space. When selling a well-loved coachbuilt model after nearly eight years, I found myself unloading tinned chickens, cocoa, and *Daily Telegraph Magazines* which had accompanied me unused from Calabria to the Canaries.

General speaking, the more manoeuvrable vans are cheaper: the more comfortable vans tend to be more expensive. Up to that 'optimum' we have just noted, therefore, it might be assumed that a purchaser should choose the most expensive van he can afford.

But this is a matter for individual choice. The mere fact of driving a vehicle worth £5,000 or more can in itself be a burden to certain temperaments. The thought of all that valuable equipment at risk is a source of constant worry to them. Others will react in a directly opposed manner, taking pride in their new possession.

In some respects, a motor caravan is nearer to a suit of clothes than to a house in the closeness of its fit, and in the intimate reflection of its owner's personality. I know a wealthy resident of the Côte d'Azur whose brown Peugeot delivery van, cosy enough inside, has no side windows and is indistinguishable from the baker's or the electrician's. But then he himself, when he steps outside, differs from the fishermen or farmers amongst whom he has parked only in that his jeans are just slightly better cut, his T-shirt just a little more recently laundered. In choosing a motor caravan, therefore, let the watchword be: 'Know thyself'.

This self analysis once begun – for only a prolonged experience of motor caravanning will complete it – the range of models available can be considered in more detail.

It will soon be noted that only a limited number of interior layouts are possible. Even in the case of coachbuilt models (Group 4) this number depends on what can be fitted into a space which rarely exceeds 6 ft wide by 6 ft high by 10 ft long. But within this space the designer has no obstacle or intrusion to take into account other than the rear wheel arches. And provided that these are covered either by a bed, a seat, or some form of cupboard, their presence is not noticed. The only occasion, in practice, when he would have to consider them would be in the positioning of a 'side-dinette'. Then the table, when in use, must not stand directly above the wheel arch, or there will be no leg room.

One or more of these 'dinettes' form the most prominent feature of most layouts. A dinette can be defined as seats for two, four, or even six people on either side of a table. The table can also be lowered to the level of the seats to form a double bed. Most common is the 'centre dinette', just behind the cab. This allows all the rear of the caravan to be devoted to working, washing, and clothes storage. A typical plan is shown below.

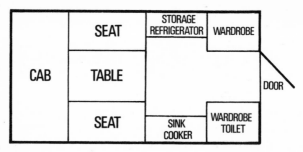

This is generally accepted to be the only practical scheme available for a rear-door model. But it does have two real advantages. It concentrates the working area near the exit, which is useful when cooking or washing-up; and secondly, it places the dining and sleeping area squarely in the centre, thus providing protection against draughts and cold outer walls in winter weather.

A variation of this formula is a feature of one of the most popular of all coachbuilt models, the CI Highwayman. The cupboards and working apparatus are replaced down one side by a settee, which pulls out to form a double bed.

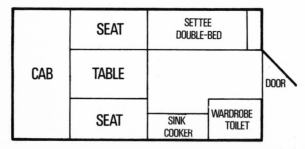

This greatly extends the vehicle's sleeping capacity. It also provides a permanent full-length mattress to stretch out on at any moment of the day or night. Anyone who has longed for a break during a tiring drive down the motorway will appreciate the value of this facility. However, storage cupboards and working surfaces are sacrificed for this extra sleeping area, and when both beds are made up there is almost no free space. This lack of space emphasizes the 'corridor living', which is very often cited as a drawback of rear-door models.

With these problems in mind a number of manufacturers over the years have introduced coachbuilt models with side doors. The early Hadrian provided an almost 'open-plan' living and sleeping area. A rear kitchen, that dream of so many trailer caravan wives, occupied two-thirds of the back wall. (The other third was filled with an unusually generously sized toilet compartment.) Then, in the mid-60s, the revolutionary Cotswold 'C' moved the dinette itself to the rear, thus cutting it right off from the engine, whilst providing an all-round view from windows on three sides. At the same time the working area remained conveniently close to the exit, and washing as well as toilet operations could be carried out in complete privacy.

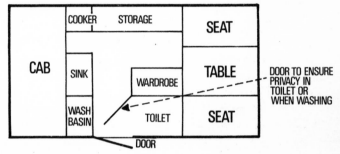

Despite the many advantages of a side door, it is bound to be hazardous when used either in Britain or on the Continent. For if placed on the near left-hand side in this country, it will necessarily open on to the road when abroad, and vice-versa. This may be one of the reasons why the larger manufacturers have been somewhat reluctant to introduce side-access to their coachbuilt models.

There are certain vans, however, which, when converted, only offer side doors. The most obvious examples are the Volkswagen 'bug' (i.e. the minibus or kombi, not the 'beetle' saloon) and the Fiat 903 cc, for their rear engines block any access from the back. They also eliminate a considerable amount of useful space, cutting down on storage room, and limiting the 'living area' to a tight square in the centre of the van.

In the case of the VW the engine height is above a comfortable level for sitting. This means either that the bed must be made up at this height when required, or that it must be formed from the seats in the centre, leaving the space above the engine to house a rather unsatisfactory assembly of small cupboards.

Rear-engined vans, such as the Volkswagen, can only be entered from the side. But well-tailored conversions, such as the Eurovette by Devon, take advantage of this to provide easy access to cooking and storage facilities from the exterior.

Problems such as these stimulate better use of the most neglected part of a van – the cab. The very fact that the engine is at the rear instead of amidships makes the cab more accessible, and some of the more recent VW conversions provide a 'walk-through' corridor between unusually comfortable driver and passenger seats. This gives the VW cab a 'sitting-room' quality, which is enhanced by its admirable draught-proof doors.

Substantial variations on the simpler layouts we have already discussed may in time be provided by the 'piggy-back' detachable unit fitting on to a pick-up chassis, which has only recently commenced manufacture in Britain. For those prepared to spend the price of a house on their motor caravan, the giant American motor homes already offer such variations. But a more important advantage of the 'piggy-backs', or 'campers' as they are called in North America, is the possibility of replacing engine and chassis, without at the same time changing the whole van.

For one of the most persuasive arguments against choosing a motor caravan in the first place has always been that an engine is likely to wear out long before the living unit mounted on it. The trailer caravanner, so the argument goes, can change his car as frequently as he wishes, while leaving intact his home on

The smallest of the Suntrekker coachbuilt detachable units fits on to the pick-up version of the BLMC Marina. As can be seen, it offers the space and comfort of motor caravans based on larger vehicles.

Once the unit is positioned on site, it releases a manoeuvrable and economic runabout.

wheels, adapted as it is to his particular requirements. But the motor caravanner can only change his entire outfit.

Some of the answers to this have already been discussed in Chapter 1. It should also be remembered that engines can be changed; while caravan bodies, too, eventually wear out. The decision to sell my second Highwayman, after nearly eight happy years, was due as much to fears for the bodywork, where loose screws had alerted me to the rotting timber of the hidden framework, as to fears for the ageing but still sturdy motor. And a diesel engine, with a lifespan of up to 200,000 miles or more, should be capable of lasting out any motor caravan.

The question of whether to use diesel or petrol, which hardly ever arose in the early days of motor caravanning, has been raised with increasing urgency as fuel prices have steadily risen, and finally rocketed. Arguments against diesel are its noise, its poor acceleration, its smell, the relative scarcity of service stations supplying diesel fuel, the even greater scarcity of diesel mechanics, the greater complexity of serious diesel repairs, and its initial cost – from £100 to £350 more than the corresponding petrol-driven model.

The advantages become apparent if we answer each of these criticisms in turn. Noise can be reduced by lagging, and is of less importance on journeys made by a motor caravan, which on the whole tend to be shorter. Diesels 'pull' better than petrol engines, and in a motor caravan their relatively slower speed matters less. Smell, on the other hand, matters even more than in a car; but I am assured that a diesel engine kept in good order will run 'clean'. Service stations which supply diesel fuel are more widespread on the Continent than in Britain; but in any case there can be few roads in any part of Europe where one can go for a hundred miles without finding one. And because diesel provides more miles per gallon than petrol, the 'autonomy' given by a tank of the same size is greater.

Major troubles, it is true, are more serious than in petrol engines, and mechanics able to cope with them are fewer on the ground. However, problems tend to arise less frequently. The engine is basically simpler, with no sparking plugs or distributor, for example, to give trouble. Remember, too, that tractor mechanics are accustomed to diesel engines. The places where serious difficulties in repair might well occur are in remoter areas of the developing countries. But in some of these, notably the Middle East, petrol is so cheap as to make a diesel engine unnecessary merely for reasons of economy.

The great argument in its favour is, of course, the economy in running. Users claim that they can obtain between one third and two thirds more miles per gallon, and although the price advantage in the UK is small, even since extra VAT was imposed on petrol, diesel is significantly cheaper almost everywhere on the Continent. Until recent price adjustments, which removed some of the differential, it cost little more than a third as much as petrol in France, in Spain, and in Portugal. Even now the diesel owner, after taking into consideration both economy in running and the price of fuel, is getting more than twice as many miles for his money in those countries.

Certain rules will soon be learned by anyone acquiring a diesel-run motor caravan. He must never allow his tank to become completely empty, because he will not then be able to restart merely by having it refilled. The whole process of starting up is also a heavier operation for this engine. Both the starter motor and the heavy-duty battery are more powerful than on an equivalent petrol model. The diesel owner, in particular, would be wise to fit an auxiliary battery to supply the internal lighting system, so that the main battery remains fully charged and ready to start up the engine.

Two other factors to be borne in mind when choosing a van concern the manufacturer of the basic vehicle. Where is the motor caravanner going to spend most time? If abroad, then he must chalk up a point in favour of such manufacturers as Volkswagen, Fiat, Renault and Peugeot, with their world-wide service facilities, and sometimes with assembly plants in several of the countries he may be likely to visit. If in Britain, then he will have yet another point to add to those in favour of British vehicles. These include not only lower prices, but more surprisingly, the greater space they generally offer for equivalent horsepower. German motor caravanners, after complaining of the 'bug's' cramped living room, poor performance at altitude, and disappointing consumption, have said to me: 'If only we had seen the Commer before we bought our Volkswagen'.

And what is the attitude of the motor manufacturer to motor caravans? This can be crucial for anyone carrying out, or paying

An elevating-roof conversion of the reliable BLMC J4, which went out of production in 1974. Its one disadvantage, like that of many smaller vans, was that it was not wide enough to accommodate transverse beds.

for, his own conversion. For some manufacturers are so uninterested, or in certain cases apparently so jealous, that on what may appear flimsy grounds they will invalidate guarantees and warranties. Chrysler (UK) and Ford have been conspicuously helpful in their promotion of their commercial vehicles for motor caravan conversion. Vauxhall now do all they can to stress the advantages of their Bedford range. British Leyland, on the other hand, seemed until recently quite uninterested, though fortunately their attitude is changing. Properly promoted the neat little J4, despite its awkward steering geometry, might in the 60s have caught up with the VW minibus, just as the dear old Morris Minor could have swept the 'beetle' saloon under the carpet back in the 50s.

Apart from discussion with enthusiasts, watch the correspondence columns and the advertisements in the motor caravanning press. Manufacturers who bother to take space to promote their vans are obviously likely to be co-operative over conversions, and helpful in the event of subsequent problems.

Probably the biggest consideration in making one's choice is that of the converter. Remember that the biggest converters have a wealth of experience, and that well-known proprietary makes have a higher second-hand value (see Chapter 5: Selling a motor caravan). Their bulk-buying of materials, and their well-organized assembly lines, can give you a lot of motor caravan for your money. But for these very reasons they can offer you only very limited variations from their standard fittings and layouts.

Smaller firms can provide a greater range of choice in these respects, and because their owners and staff may be practising motor caravanners, they often supply an understanding, as well as a personal touch, which many customers value. Auto-Sleepers, for example, is a well-established firm which retains these qualities. Richard Holdsworth has climbed into the big league by skilful use of these same qualities. The motor caravanner who is prepared to accept a non-proprietary van may find himself highly satisfied by a skilled specialist converter like Howard-Lange, who regard every new client as an individual case.

Before a final choice is made, there is much to be said in favour of hiring a van. Apart from testing the particular model chosen, this is a means of trying out the idea of motor caravanning in general. The member or members of the family who are already sold on it will probably not require this experiment, but it can help in securing the co-operation of those who may be less enthusiastic.

At the time of writing, Self Drive Hire charges vary from around £40 per week for elevating-roof models in low season, to over £100 for one of the more expensive coachbuilt models in high season. Equipment such as bedding and crockery generally forms an extra charge, but the big item of insurance is included.

3 Making your own motor caravan

by John Hunt, Editor of *Motor Caravan + Camping*

It is tempting to consider the financial advantages of making your own motor caravan from a commercial van or chassis. If you have a reasonable degree of skill with ordinary hand tools and possess an electric drill and a few attachments, it will obviously be cheaper to do the conversion yourself than to pay someone else to do it. You will not charge yourself for labour, nor will you have expensive offices to finance and public relations staff to employ. You will not have to allow a profit margin so that wholesalers and retailers can be given a 'cut', nor will you need to provide 'demonstration' vans for customers and the gentlemen of the press. Your overheads, in a word, will be nil. A 'private conversion' works out a lot cheaper than an equivalent 'professional' motor caravan conversion. I know; I have carried out several myself.

Nevertheless, my first piece of advice to those about to embark on such a project is 'don't!' There are snags. If you carve a new vehicle about, the manufacturer's guarantee may be invalidated. Unless you are very good with tools, the finished product will look obviously home-made. Some materials used by the specialists are impossible to obtain locally in small quantities. You are bound to make mistakes which could prove expensive. When you come to sell your pride and joy, the dealers will just not want to know about it. It is far more sensible to buy a good second-hand proprietary motor caravan and build in your own modifications.

Worst of all, once you have been bitten by the do-it-yourself bug, you are contaminated for life. You will never be able to resist looking at delivery vans, furniture vans, coaches even, without planning a motor caravan layout inside. A journey by bus will produce ridiculous flights of fancy – imagine going *upstairs* to bed!

If the foregoing paragraphs have not dissuaded you, read on, for you are already infected and beyond hope of cure – as I am. After some years spent towing trailer tents and caravans – and several enjoyable holidays – the motor caravan obsession is as strong as ever. Tents and caravans are all right for holidays but, as Henry Myhill will have convinced you, motor caravanning is a way of life that encompasses 365 days of each year.

As this is written, motor caravan conversion number eight is being planned in detail – and that with a comfortable car and trailer caravan in the drive outside!

Tax and private conversions

The cheapest way to make a motor caravan is to install your futnire in a commercial van without side windows. You *may* not then have to pay Car Tax (depending on the attitude of your local Customs Officer) but you *will* be refused admission to many camp sites and membership of most clubs.

Since the infamous 'Silly Billy' Budget of 1975, when differential rates of VAT were applied, motor caravans have become subject to both Car and Value Added Taxes. The private converter will automatically be charged VAT when he buys his equipment, sometimes at the basic and sometimes at the 'luxury' rate. His local Officer of Customs and Excise (address in phone book) will estimate the amount of Car Tax payable.

It is advisable to show the Customs man a rough plan of your intentions before you begin. It used to be possible to avoid Car Tax by conforming to certain requirements (a wardrobe, 6 gallons of water storage, a 6 ft bed etc), but such concessions are no longer made. The Customs man will estimate by how much you have increased the value of the vehicle – and charge you accordingly. So you can put in – or leave out – whatever equipment you wish.

Which vehicle?

First, then, is the choice of basic vehicle. All British manufacturers produce what they call a 'light delivery van', which shares engine and other components with cars in the medium price and size range. There are also imported equivalents. Vans between about 15 and 25 cwt capacity are the most popular with professional and amateur converters alike. They are reasonably car-like to drive and yet have the space to allow for a workable caravan layout.

Going up in size are the slightly larger and much more

expensive 'small heavy goods vehicles'. The gain in interior space does not appear to be justified by the terrific price difference and, once you abandon the Bedford CF, Commer 1500–2500, Ford Transit, Leyland Light Van or VW Kombi for something larger, you no longer have a 'car' which can be parked like other cars – in a meter bay, for instance. Delivery vans are seldom longer than their equivalent cars but there is much more room inside.

Nomads who are after the greatest amount of cubic footage within a given overall length will look twice at 'coachbuilt' vehicles. These are bodies which have been built by specialists on delivery-van chassis. They begin life as 'minibuses', parcels, small furniture, box or gown vans or ambulances. Buying a minibus or an ambulance new (if you could get it) would be a waste of money. You would be unlikely to recoup the full cost of the unwanted seats, stretchers and other equipment. Minibuses a year or two old are a good bet. Ambulances are usually only sold when they are becoming too expensive to maintain. Vans can reach the second-hand market at all times and for all reasons, and are worth searching for. Bargains are to be had, but choose a vehicle which has had a kind first owner – a baker rather than a builder!

There is a growing interest in large vehicles for motor caravan conversion, but, unless you have some knowledge of them, they could prove to be an expensive mistake. At least cut your teeth on something fairly standard.

Small vehicles are also increasing in popularity but conversion of a CDV (car-derived van) poses problems not confined to layout. Some Customs officers do not like them – so read on.

Interior layout

Many evenings can be spent discussing with the family the position of seats, beds, table, wardrobe, toilet compartment. A sheet of squared paper will be useful – and a rubber! More ambitious converters will make scale models in cardboard, with furniture units which can be moved around until everyone is happy.

There are certain minimum sizes. One bed must be 6 ft long. Anything less than 2 ft in width will be inadequate – 2 ft 3 in is preferable. Strangely enough, 4 ft seems generous for a double bed and you could get by with 3 ft 6 in. The wardrobe should be wide enough to take an ordinary coat hanger (18 in) and deep enough to allow a drop of about 30 in.

If you have read this far, you will doubtless have looked with interest at other motor caravans and will have come to realize that it is customary to build seats (which must double as beds) with lockers beneath, in which clothes and bedding are stored. For maximum storage space, a layout with a single bed along each wall is the simplest arrangement. But some of today's delivery vans are only 7 ft 6 in long inside and, with 6 ft for each bed, 1 ft 6 in is not going to be enough for cooker, sink and wardrobe.

Or is it? You may have other ideas. That is the beauty of doing it yourself. You do not have to copy a professional conversion, which has been designed anyway with more than half an eye on showroom appeal. User convenience then comes a very poor second.

If you want more room in the van body for the kitchen unit and wardrobe, the seats could be arranged so that you sleep with your feet in the driving cab. This would involve incorporating cab seats with backs that fold right down. Some specialist motor caravan builders might be willing to supply them.

Alternatively, if the van is wide enough, a double bed could be arranged across the vehicle behind the cab. This would save 2 ft or so of space occupied by the bed. This is the arrangement favoured by the majority of converters. The rear seats face inwards, with a table between. At night, the table is dropped to rest between the seat bases and cushions are rearranged to make the mattress.

This emphasizes another mistake which I made on my own first conversion. All cushions were the same size: 1 ft 6 in – because 4 × 1 ft 6 in equals 6 ft. It is better to do the sum another way: 2 × 2 ft plus 2 × 1 ft. The smaller cushions make backrests during the day.

If you often carry passengers, they may want to sit facing forwards when travelling. If the inward-facing seats and their supporting lockers are each split into two, cushions can be arranged to give two single forward-facing seats. Or a different arrangement of cushions could provide a three- or four-seater settee across the body of the van.

Interesting variations on layout are possible if the van has a side door and the seats/beds are placed at the rear. The possibilities are endless and will stretch your ingenuity to the utmost.

Insulation and sound proofing

You will want your caravan to be as quiet as possible on the road and comfortably warm on site. Sound proofing needs heavy materials. Thick carpet felt will work. The purpose-made materials supplied by automobile sound-proofing specialists are probably more efficient. Use as much as you can afford or squeeze in on the cab floor, engine bulkhead and wheel arches – especially if they protrude into the cab. The floor of the van should also be completely covered.

Walls and roofs need a lighter-weight material. Flame-retardant expanded polystyrene works. Glass-fibre wool, as sold for insulating lofts in houses, is probably better, but will need fastening at intervals to prevent sagging. At least one DIY man swears by crumpled newspaper behind the interior panels of his caravan. There are also foam injection materials now available from glass-fibre manufacturers.

A fixed roof (high-top or original van roof) should be lined with thin ply or hardboard so that it is double skinned, like the walls. Insulating material is packed into the cavity.

A proprietary elevating roof poses an insulation problem. Automobile sound-proofing suppliers sell self-adhesive materials by the yard, and this can be stuck on the underside of the rigid top panel. I have found that the quilted material sold by Woolworths is suitable for lining the flexible sides. It cuts down heat losses considerably, but does make closing the roof a little more bothersome.

Ventilation is as important as insulation. Trailer caravans must, by law, have certain ventilators which cannot be closed. Motor caravans, which are often smaller, need them. There should be some in the floor (away from exhaust fumes), and some in walls or roof. *Motor Caravan + Camping* receives regular complaints from readers about condensation inside vans, not only on windows. Often an adequate supply of floor-to-roof ventilation will alleviate or cure the trouble. Whilst the gas we use is non-toxic, a certain amount of carbon monoxide can result from combustion, plus a great deal of water vapour, which must be dispersed. What is more, a gas flame is hungry for oxygen, and is no respecter of the demands of the human body.

Windows and roofs

Only the most ambitious will consider making their own window frames. These are available retail from many caravan suppliers in every type of design. Glass may need to be ordered and fitted locally. It is essential to specify safety glass (trailer caravan windows are of ordinary sheet glass).

Cutting the apertures for the windows does require a special tool – a metal shearer (a cross between pliers and tinsnips and worked by hand), or a nibbler to fit your electric drill. In some localities it is possible to hire these tools (the telephone directory will give the names of 'hire shops'). Before you begin cutting, make brown paper templates of the areas to be cut out and stick them in position on the outside of the van with a paste that can be washed off. Drill a hole (not less than $\frac{1}{4}$ in) at each corner and cut in straight lines between the holes. Corners should always be left rounded and never cut 'square', which could lead to splitting. If by some mischance you end up with a square corner, make it round again with a file.

If you are going to raise the roof (either permanently or just when you camp), the aperture is cut in the same way as for the windows. Here follows a very important warning: **build in as much strength as you take out**! Modern vans, like cars, seldom have proper chassis, and removing part of the body can weaken the whole structure.

Commercial converters will remove practically the whole of the roof, down to the gutter. They have knowledge, equipment for strengthening, and vehicle manufacturer's approval. Amateurs are advised to leave in place most of the curved part above the guttering at sides and rear and the whole of the roof of the cab. Even so, when you have removed the roof panel, your van will have about as much strength as a wet cornflakes packet. Don't drive it!

If you buy an elevating roof, the size of the aperture will be decided for you and the necessary strengthening supplied. I do not recommend making your own elevating roof, unless you are more than averagely competent. I'm not. I've tried. I wish I hadn't.

A high-top is easy to make. The simplest, and probably the strongest type, is a curved one with flat sides, which are bolted to the van above the guttering. The curved top can be of aluminium or waterproof ply, suitably reinforced with cross members from side to side. The gentle curve gives strength.

Furniture

It is, of course, cheaper to make all your own furniture – and the cheapest, but most time consuming, method is to make frames of $1\frac{1}{2} \times 1$ in planed timber, clad on one side with hardboard or three-ply wood. Doors should be clad on both sides to avoid warping.

A simpler way to construct the furniture units is to make everything of chipboard, or the veneered chipboard which is sold under various trade names. This will render most of the tedious framing unnecessary. It helps to cover the whole floor of the van with a sheet of chipboard, preferably over insulating felt. Furniture units can be screwed to this rather than direct to the van's metal floor. Do not forget to drill the necessary holes for waste outlet and water and gas inlet points before installing. Chain stores sell a useful little holesaw with interchangeable blades, which is ideal for the job. The large holes in the metal floor can be made with a 'tank cutter'; an alternative method is to drill little holes all round the circumference (chain drilling) and file the rough edge smooth.

Bases for seats/beds are usually constructed with hinged or removable tops to provide easy access to the lockers below. It helps to make only about three quarters of the top removable. Cushions can then be stood on their edges on the remaining fixed quarter while you ferret around for whatever is needed from the locker. A stay to hold up the lid would be useful.

More expensive, rather untidy, but so much more convenient, are seat bases hinged to the walls and supported on legs, leaving sides open. The space beneath the seat is then occupied by purpose-made, pull-out storage boxes. When necessary, the boxes may be removed entirely, the seats hinged up and held against the walls, and the clear floor space used for carrying loads. Provided the seats are not removed from the caravan you will not be contravening regulations, but do make sure that insurance is still valid.

Furniture units designed specifically for certain basic vans are becoming increasingly popular. These, with window and roof kits, are available from several firms, who also build complete motor caravans for sale. You buy what you need: a kitchen or a wardrobe unit, for instance, or everything required to convert your commercial van into a fully fledged motor caravan – roof, windows, lining, furniture, curtain runners, water tank. Many firms install the difficult parts, such as roof and windows, for you.

Plumbing: gas and water

Unless you are aiming to be entirely individualistic, heating within the caravan – and cooling, if you plan to have a refrigerator – will be by bottled gas or LPG (liquefied petroleum gas, not 'low pressure gas' as some caravanners think). It comes in two forms: butane and propane. Butane is cheaper and more readily available, but propane vaporizes at a lower temperature. If you plan to camp in winter, propane is advisable. Gas cylinders or 'bottles' come in all sorts of shapes and sizes. The 6 lb and 10 lb sizes are the most popular for motor caravan installation, although some of the larger 'motor homes' can carry bigger ones.

The first golden rule is to arrange for the gas bottles to be stowed in a place where they cannot fall over. They must be kept upright, with regulators at the tops. The second, and equally vital, rule is to ensure that the gas bottle locker is adequately ventilated *downwards*, because gas is heavier than air.

The regulator on the gas bottle in use should be connected to the van's gas piping system by a length of flexible pipe bought from an LPG supplier specifically for the purpose. Any old bit of hose just will not do.

Every do-it-yourself enthusiast can be his own gas plumber nowadays. Blow torches and sweated joints are things of the past. All that is needed is a hacksaw, a small file and a spanner of the right size – and a bit of washing-up liquid to search for leaks at each joint when you first test the system. Most caravan accessory shops and boat chandlers sell copper gas piping and fittings. Calor Gas publish recommendations on installation and use.

Obviously, gas plumbing must be done with care – and neatly. Pipe runs should be secured at intervals to prevent movement and possible fracture through metal fatigue. If pipes run underneath the vehicle, try to ensure that they are located where flying stones will not strike them, and where they are out of reach of ham-fisted garage mechanics.

There is no reliable indication of exactly when the gas bottle will run out, but you can rely on its being at the most inconvenient time imaginable. For this reason I recommend that a gas-operated refrigerator should be supplied by its own bottle, and not piped into the system that operates cooker, heater, lights etc. The fridge will be 'on' when motoring and at night. At such times it is advisable to turn all other appliances off at the 'mains'.

Many motorists do not like driving with a gas flame alight, in spite of the almost universal use on refrigerators of flame failure devices, which automatically turn off the gas if the flame goes out. They will need a gas/12 volt electric model and should not forget to switch over to gas operation when in camp. All-electric refrigerators are a thing of the not-too-distant future.

It is useful to have a space heater of some sort. If your camping is mainly confined to the summer months, a cheap little radiant or convector heater will suffice. For winter nomads something more permanent is desirable. The 'catalytic' heaters are excellent because they have no flame, are non-toxic and need no flue. Many have oxygen analysers, which turn off the appliance if there is insufficient air in the van.

Of course, any gas fire must be sited where it is not a hazard. To warm the van it needs to be low down, and that is just where trailing clothes can catch it. If the dress guard seems inadequate, make a better one with diamond mesh.

The latest idea is a blown hot-air system, the heat coming from gas and the forced draught from an electric fan, operated by the vehicle's battery. The advantage is that hot air can be piped to all parts of the van – a true central-heating system.

Water plumbing can be as simple or as sophisticated as you like. Obviously the simplest method is to use a bowl, which is filled from a portable container, but most motor caravans are now fitted with a sink, and water is pumped from a portable container or a fitted tank. The waste pipe from the sink discharges into a bucket underneath the van. A sophisticated water system will have both a fresh- and a waste-water tank, with an electric pump to feed water to the sink. 'Instant' gas water heaters can be incorporated and will supply not only the sink, but the toilet room and shower head with mixer taps. A pump is essential here, for it is impracticable and inadvisable to use a header tank. Such a system would need a pressure-sensitive switch for the pump, so that when any tap is turned on, the pump begins to work.

Water plumbing is normally carried out in polythene tubing of about $\frac{1}{2}$ in internal diameter. It can be bought, together with necessary fittings, at caravan accessory shops. If possible, obtain black polythene tubing and water tanks. Light is excluded and the formation of algae inhibited. Do not economize by using coloured garden hose. Some of the dyes used are toxic.

Electricity

It is important to remember that cable should be sufficiently heavy. Ordinary domestic lighting flex is not suitable. It's the amperage that matters and it is helpful to remember the old formula:

$$\text{amps} = \frac{\text{watts}}{\text{volts}}$$

With mains voltage of 240 and a 60 watt lamp, amperage will be $60 \div 240$, or only $\frac{1}{4}$. With but 12 volts, a 60 watt lamp (e.g. a headlamp) will demand 5 amps. A fluorescent tube giving the same amount of light as a 60 watt bulb will be rated at about 18 watts, and will consume about $1\frac{1}{2}$ amps. This is an over-simplification and there are other factors to be taken into account. With low-voltage direct current, voltage drop is considerable over comparatively short runs of cable. The thicker the cable the less the drop.

Since most motor caravanners use the vehicle's battery to supply interior lighting, the reason for the current popularity of fluorescent lamps, with their comparatively low consumption, is obvious. I do not think it is necessary to install a second battery purely for running two or three fluorescent lamps, provided there is a reasonable amount of motoring between stops. When camped for several days, running the engine for a while each day will keep a good battery 'topped up'. But if you camp during the winter's long dark evenings, run a water pump and television set, then it is worth the expense. You will need a blocking diode or a split-charge relay, so that the second battery, if low, does not rob the main battery of its charge, making it impossible to start the engine the next day. Such a device will also ensure that the vehicle's battery gets first call on the alternator. Blocking diodes and split-charge relays come with full wiring instructions.

As a compromise, and if the space is available, it might be worth considering buying the biggest possible battery that can be fitted. It is a lot simpler than running two batteries.

Do not, when considering interior lighting, dismiss the idea of gas lamps as old fashioned. They have advantages: (a) if there is an alternative source of lighting, you will never be completely in the dark, and batteries have been known to fail without warning; (b) gas lamps give a warm glow – welcome on a cold night; (c) fluorescent lamps can set up interference on portable radios.

Mains electricity is commonly available to caravanners on the Continent, but is much less so in Britain. If you propose wiring the van for a 'mains hook-up', do get professional advice. The Institution of Electrical Engineers sell a useful book of recommendations.

Miniature motor caravanning

With the inevitable upward trend in the price of petrol, the idea of squeezing a quart into a pint pot becomes intriguing. Conventional light delivery vans of 10–20 cwt capacity return a fuel consumption of around 18–24 mpg. A car-derived van of 8–10 cwt will top 30 mpg, and sometimes approach 40 in favourable conditions.

The conversion of the interior of a CDV calls for a great deal of ingenuity. On a miniature conversion of a Ford CDV, I built my own punt-shaped elevating roof, which stuck out over the bonnet, giving a total length of 9 ft. The roof was front hinged and the first 6 ft were occupied by a double bed, which could be left permanently made up. Access to the bed was via a ladder from the interior of the van. The whole of the 'downstairs' part could thus be given over to seating and other caravan necessities. Room was available to carry a large chemical closet and there was no problem about stowage of bedding – a space-consuming item in all motor caravans. It did look odd though!

Information and sources

With the growth of all types of caravanning, materials for conversion are easier to come by every year. Most trailer-caravan dealers sell sinks and stoves and other equipment for furnishing interiors. Readers who live near the coast or a waterway should explore the stocks of boat chandlers. It is surprising how many fittings boats and caravans have in common.

I have studiously avoided mentioning names in this chapter, but there is one that must be allowed to creep in: Joy and King of North London are real specialists and their catalogue is a treasure trove. Now, having broken my self-imposed embargo, here follow a few more names.

The Auto Camping Club runs a DIY service for members (with which I am associated) and sells some helpful publications: *DIY Directory*, containing hundreds of addresses of DIY suppliers; *Make Yourself a Motor Caravan*, by yours truly; as well as plans and detailed instructions for conversion of some popular vehicles. The Motor Caravanners' Club publishes a comprehensive 'DIY Dossier' based on members' experiences. Advice on certain aspects is also obtainable from the Caravan Club and the Camping Club of Great Britain and Ireland.

The caravanning press and *Exchange and Mart* contain some useful advertisements. Although I shouldn't, in modesty, admit it, the magazine with the strongest regular DIY section for motor caravanners is – you guessed? – *Motor Caravan + Camping*. The editorial office also keeps a list of addresses of readers who have carried out conversions or modifications and are willing to share their experiences.

Some useful addresses for DIY enthusiasts
JOHN HUNT, Editor, *Motor Caravan + Camping*, c/o 104 St Luke's Road, Old Windsor, Berks
AUTO CAMPING CLUB: 5 Dunsfold Rise, Coulsdon, Surrey CR3 2ED
CALOR GAS LTD: Calor Gas House, Key West, Windsor Road, Slough, Bucks
CAMPING CLUB OF GREAT BRITAIN & IRELAND: 11 Lower Grosvenor Place, London SW1W 0EY
CARAVAN CLUB: 65 South Molton Street, London W1Y 2AB
INSTITUTION OF ELECTRICAL ENGINEERS: Savoy Place, Victoria Embankment, London WC2R 0BL
JOY & KING LTD: 15 Alperton Lane, Perivale, Greenford, Middx
MOTOR CARAVANNERS' CLUB: 29 Wimbledon Park Road, London SW18 5SJ
SOUND SERVICES (OXFORD) LTD: 55 West End, Witney, Oxon

4 Insurance

The first motor caravans were insured as vans in private use. This is still more or less the situation today, but there was an awkward period in between, as insurance companies gradually realized that a new vehicle had appeared on the roads, which was neither car, nor van, nor trailer caravan.

Some owners had difficulty in obtaining cover from their traditional insurers, or were only granted it because they were long-standing and valued clients. On the other hand skilful and helpful brokers, who knew their way round the insurance market, were able to offer preferential terms to members of such organizations as the Motor Caravanners' Club.

But London is the insurance capital of the world. Provision for the new vehicle was soon made, especially after statistics began to show that its accident rate tended to be below average. This is probably because the sensation of driving a motor caravan is different from that of driving a car. It is not merely a machine for moving in, but a machine for living in. Researchers into accident prevention discovered some years ago that if owners thought of their cars less as instruments of speed and self-expression, and more as homes on wheels, their whole style of driving would change for the better. Only after they had reached this conclusion was it pointed out that their 'ideal car' already existed – the motor caravan.

It would be too much to expect that, because of this inherent tendency to safer driving, the motor caravanner should actually pay less premium than the average motorist. In the case of a fully comprehensive policy, he is bound to pay more because of the greater value of bodywork and equipment exposed to fire, theft, and accident. But at least he is no longer unduly penalized.

Only the individual can decide how much insurance above the official minimum he requires. A good insurance broker can give advice, and knows where to find the best terms. Special terms for motor caravanners, offered to members of various organizations, are always worth considering, although they should be compared with policies available to the general public to see just how substantial their advantages are.

Insurance abroad involves several other factors. Within the Common Market a Green Card is, strictly speaking, no longer required. However, the cover provided on existing policies by British insurance companies, in order to conform to the Treaty of Rome, is the barest minimum for each country concerned. Generally it covers liability for bodily injury only. Denting a parked Mercedes can lead to a hefty bill!

Any additional cover within the EEC, and within those countries outside, like Switzerland, which have now adhered to the same insurance agreement, and any cover at all in other countries, necessitates a Green Card. Fifteen years ago this used to be provided free on demand for up to three months. Then a fee of two guineas was charged to cover the cost of the paperwork. Now a substantial extra premium is asked, often as much as 80% of that already paid for cover in the UK.

Extension of the Green Card for a further three months, once almost a formality, is now increasingly difficult to negotiate. For despite London's reputation in insurance, and the increasing integration of Europe, repair costs abroad are substantially higher, and even more difficult to 'vet'.

Motor caravanners leaving Britain for long periods might therefore consider taking out an Overseas Policy, renewable annually, which provides a Green Card valid for twelve months. At the time of writing the Caledonian, a member of the Guardian Royal Exchange Assurance Group, is the only company which offers this particular service.

Remember that an Overseas Policy covering a British-registered vehicle is only valid in Britain when a 'white' Certificate of Insurance has been provided, as distinct from the Green Card.

Premiums on fully comprehensive Overseas Policies are so high that in certain circumstances the motor caravanner may prefer to pay for 'Third Party' cover only. For example, an older, British van would have a low replacement value in the event of total loss, yet would be most unlikely to be stolen. For how long would a Frenchman be able to travel in a dilapidated right-hand drive Highwayman without inviting suspicion?

An Overseas Policy will generally cover most European countries, and these will be individually listed in the actual policy. Certain countries, however, such as Bulgaria and Morocco, may require a separate arrangement, and the payment of an extra premium. Alternatively, insurance may be purchased in such countries at the frontier, either from private agencies, or from the state. In a number of places, in Algeria for example, where Green Cards are not accepted, frontier insurance is the only type available. It is sold for limited periods, such as seven, seventeen, or thirty days, and can prove to be expensive, unless one is careful to limit one's stay to within the period chosen.

However, there are particular countries where at certain times frontier insurance has been a 'best buy'. Purchasers of Spain's State Tourist Insurance, for example, have often been able to obtain good cover at a reasonable price, and the assurance that they, at least, would not be put into prison after an accident until the police had made sure that their liabilities would be paid in full.

So consult your broker. And above all, keep your ears open when with other motor caravanners!

5 Selling a motor caravan

Selling anything is on the whole more difficult than buying it. Selling some new, little-known and generally misunderstood product is inevitably more difficult still. So it is not surprising that the market in second-hand motor caravans got off to a sticky start.

One recalls the unrealistic figures quoted in advertisements by proud pioneering owners, who had dreamed up yet another conversion, or by 'failed motor caravanners', who had poured money into some pet dream, only to be disappointed by the reality. And one recalls too, that the actual price for which these vans finally changed hands, was often very different from the original asking price.

Two developments lifted the market off the ground. One was demand from overseas visitors. The other was the need for dealers to find buyers for second-hand vans if their first owners were ever to purchase replacements.

In the case of the first and biggest dealer of all, the two developments went hand in hand. Already in the very early 60s Wilsons of Brixton were advertizing second-hand as well as new models in the few periodicals where there was the slightest chance of a market. Response came not from the firm's pre-motor caravanning catchment area of South London, but from all over the provinces, and from visitors to Europe from North America, Southern Africa and Australasia. Wilsons took the obvious step of approaching these markets directly, by placing advertisements in provincial, American and Commonwealth newspapers. Following up this success, Wilsons first provincial showroom was opened at Bradford in 1966, and others were opened at Epsom in 1970 and at Castle Donington in 1971. Wilsons did not actually have showrooms overseas, but they did create markets there with the help of publicity derived from such innovations as a promotional motor caravan tour of Australia.

Even in the early 60s Wilsons were not alone. An honoured place already belonged to Turners of Dulwich, and since then the number of dealers, whether with single or multiple show-rooms, has grown far more rapidly than that of the converters.

Be it in non-ferrous metals, greengroceries or motor caravans, the 'middle man' is never free from criticisms. These criticisms are directed in the first place at his margins. At first sight these may seem excessive. Your van, sold, for example, at less than £500, may be almost immediately offered for sale at £899. Surely even the most notorious second-hand car dealers could not do better – or worse – than that? But there are several points to be made in the dealer's favour.

In the first place, what were you originally asking for your van? A good deal more than £485? But, of course, you were prepared to come down. So is the dealer. Judge him on the actual price he receives, and be prepared to barter with him, as much when buying as when selling. In the second place, remember that he did buy your van, and gave you hard cash for it at a time when not one of the non-specialist garages you tried would look at it. He will have to finance that purchase, perhaps for many months, at a time possibly of high interest rates. In increasing your liquidity he has reduced his own. For these last three reasons he could have afforded to give you better terms, if, as part of the deal, you had purchased another van. The fact is that the dealer is giving you the convenience of a ready-made market.

Now a market is simply a piece of machinery, whereby ready buyer meets ready seller. The greater the numbers of the product being exchanged, and the more the middle men, the better the market, and the narrower the margins. There may be only 2p between the buying and the selling price of ICI shares on the Stock Exchange. And if you think you can do better 'outside the market', whether for your shares or for your motor caravan, the choice is yours. But you will not get many replies to a 'small ad' in the *Financial Times* offering your ICIs at a price 30% above that on the quotations page in the same edition.

However, such a 'small ad' for your second-hand motor caravan in *Exchange and Mart* may find quite a few takers. You and the potential purchaser may both be better satisfied 'out-side the market', because you can agree on a price somewhere within the margins which the dealer has to keep wide for many justifiable reasons.

One of these reasons only dates from the introduction of Value Added Tax. A dealer has to pay this on every sale which he makes whether new or second-hand. Transactions between private individuals are exempted. This automatically gives the private seller a built-in advantage, to add to his freedom from overheads – showroom, salesmen, stock-financing and the rest.

Where then should he advertise? Apart from the unique *Exchange and Mart* there is the specialist press. This consists in the first place of *Motor Caravan + Camping*, the only national motor caravan journal on sale to the public, and *The Motor Caravanner*, the privately circulated monthly of the Motor Caravanners' Club. There is also a motor caravanning, or, more important still, a potential motor caravanning element amongst the readership of journals such as *Caravan*, *Modern Caravan*, *The Autocar*, *Practical Camping*, and so on.

Finally, there is the local press. An insertion in your provincial evening paper, or weekly advertiser, can often produce the fastest results. A local telephone call, a short drive, a friendly chat over tea or coffee brewed up in the van itself, and the deal is often settled. There will be no commission to pay, no 'mark up' to be allowed for, and no long journeys for inspection or delivery.

These advantages of private sales apply to all motor caravans. But they are particularly valid for non-proprietary makes. For the well-known models by established manufacturers – CI Autohomes, Dormobile, Auto-Sleeper, and so on – have now received the apotheosis of quotation in *Glass's Guide to Used Car Prices*, where each receives a valuation according to its year of make. *Glass's*, of course, is not available to the general public, but this means that a dealer buying one knows where he stands, and has some guarantee of his money back.

He has no such guarantee with a specially-converted, or self-converted van, however brilliant the design, and however good the materials, and workmanship. If he decides to buy it, he will therefore offer a lower price than for a corresponding proprietary model, just as an insurance company, if it decides to invest in a private, unquoted company, will expect its shares at a substantial discount on those of an equivalent public company, to compensate for their reduced marketability.

This ultimate marketability, when the time comes to change or to sell, is of course one of the prime considerations to have in mind when choosing a van. Likewise, anyone searching for a second-hand van should not only keep his eye on the advertisements in all the magazines mentioned, but should also keep in touch with a dealer. For the dealer may quite conceivably have a replacement customer whose van, for any of the above reasons, he does not wish to take on his books, but for which he is only too eager to find a buyer.

It is obvious that the best time for buying a used van is the worst possible moment to sell one. This 'dead' season comes with the onset of cold weather, from early October. It is then not only British residents who are wondering whether to dispose of the vans they have used throughout the summer, but also overseas visitors, who have been touring Europe for six months, and are preparing to return home. The already overloaded market is further depressed by those dealers who seek to sell off their hire fleets, together with those vans which they sold to Americans or Australians at Easter on a 'guaranteed buy-back' basis.

On the other hand, April, and even May, are often too early for a good sale. It is in June that the market really takes off, reaching a peak in early July, when demand from British holidaymakers is suddenly added to that from America and the old Commonwealth. From then on the demand falls off, but there are certain geographical exceptions. In seaside resorts, for example, hoteliers and shopkeepers take their own holidays when others have returned home. A van which suits their requirements will find a ready buyer in August or even September. And if they have had a good season they may not even argue too much about the price!

6 Heating and ventilation

The second part of this guide discusses the various aspects of living in a motor caravan: what to eat, how to sleep, how to keep clean, what to wear, how to extend one's living space by annexes, how to extend one's range of experience by accessories and how to extend one's range of travel by auxiliary transport. There is one aspect of life in a motor caravan which is of even greater importance – temperature.

The two essential instruments for achieving the right temperature are neither fires nor heaters, but insulation and ventilation. They have already been discussed by John Hunt in Chapter 3, 'Making your own motor caravan'. As regards insulation I shall mention only two points, neither of which was within his terms of reference. One is the useful role which can be played by curtains – and not only at the windows. For windows, although thin, and unless double-glazed exposed to heat-loss and condensation, are not particularly draughty. But doors are. Curtains across the back or side door, or between the cab and the living unit, can make a van much cosier. They must be sufficiently thick, and ideally should be lined.

The other is what might be called seasonal insulation. Carpeting, for example, though so warm under foot in winter, is unnecessary and often a nuisance in summer. So why not cut a square of carpet to fit exactly into the floor space of the dinette? This is where it is really needed in winter, and the area for working and washing is then left bare, so that it can easily be brushed or wiped. In summer, the square can be rolled up, slipped into a polythene bag, and stowed at the back of the luton.

The rooflights, too, which in cold weather may cause a steady drip of water from condensation, can be fitted with panels of expanded polystyrene. Although this material is semi-translucent, it does give the van a cosier feel in winter, and the panels can be removed to let in more light in the summer.

The merits of ventilation were illustrated by my second Highwayman. Provided that there was the very faintest of breezes – and rare indeed is the day without one – its four smallish windows and its large rooflight kept it cooler inside than the air outside even under a blazing sun.

This may be the best moment to introduce a reference to mosquito netting, which can make an enormous difference to comfort inside a van in summer. For windows and rooflights netting should be fastened to detachable wooden or aluminium frames. For doors a length of cotton, rather than nylon, netting can be weighted down by a strip of wood, either attached to the bottom, or to keep it in position. Some people also find that strands of coloured plastic, or lengths of wooden beads are equally satisfactory.

John Hunt has already discussed individual stoves and heaters, and the butane and propane gas which operates them. Remember that although catalytic heaters are efficient and non-toxic, they are up to eight times more expensive than simple gas fires. Consider, too, if you are going to do a lot of winter travelling, the advantages of a specially fitted heater which draws in a supply of fresh air from the exterior.

If you are going to spend long periods abroad, there is much to be said in favour of using the 3 kilogram 'blue bottles' of the French Camping Gaz, rather than a British brand. It is more expensive. But the company's full name is Camping Gaz International, and its availability really is almost worldwide. British bottles, on the other hand, must be filled up at one of the rare liquid-gas filling stations.

For some reason Camping Gaz bottles, and their refills, are only about a third of the price in Spain than anywhere else. So wait until you cross the Pyrenees before you purchase your spare second and third bottles. And make sure you cross the frontier on your way north again with a fresh set of refills – it will even pay you to exchange one which is only half full.

Several supplementary sources of heat are available to the motor caravanner. The most obvious is sunshine. On fine autumn days in Britain, or winter days on the Mediterranean, bright clear sunlight is succeeded by a bitterly cold night. Closing the doors and windows an hour or so before sunset will build up enough heat to keep the van warm for roughly the same length of time after dark. If you then start to cook dinner, it will be almost bedtime before a stove seems necessary. For the heat from cooking is sufficient to warm up the limited cubic space of the average van.

People who are used to a saloon car often complain of the noise of a motor caravan's engine, situated between driver and passenger. But the heat given off is sufficient to keep a van warm during a halt for lunch in winter. It also forms an ideal radiator for drying clothes during wet weather.

A useful stopgap for those without a stove is a plant pot or a firebrick placed over a gas ring. The firebrick will even continue to radiate heat after the flame is extinguished. Finally, do not despise that old-fashioned portable heater: the hot-water bottle.

The best of all solutions to the motor caravanner's winter heating problem is simpler still, and not as expensive as it sounds. It is to drive south – to a warmer climate.

7 Cooking and food

Two types of person will derive an uncovenanted pleasure from many aspects of motor caravanning. One is the man or woman whose natural preference for austerity and simplification receives its supreme justification in this restricted space. The other is the gadget enthusiast, who can here indulge his passion for three-in-one tools, inflatable cushions, and other devices which would never be tolerated in a normal home.

Both types find scope with regard to food and cooking. Both types, too, have something in their favour, provided they steer clear of the extremes of squalor on the one hand, and such adjuncts as electric mixers running off the battery on the other. But most motor caravanners, and most lady caravanners in particular, like their kitchen on wheels to resemble as closely as possible their kitchen at home.

The manufacturers are aware of this, and do everything they can to provide the basic fittings. The alterations a buyer can successfully make after purchase are limited. So early attention should be given to the fixtures in any particular conversion, and to the alternatives offered.

The most frequently offered choice is between a complete oven, with grill and burners, and a grill/burner, with a refrigerator in place of the oven. This brings us to the question of whether an oven and a refrigerator are essential features of a motor caravan. Leaving the refrigerator until later, except to say that more people insist on it than upon an oven, and that few vans really have the space for both, I shall here go out on a limb and assert that a fixed oven is dispensable. This is partly because caravan cooking makes fewer demands on the oven. There tend to be fewer roasts with two veg., fewer pies, fewer baked apples, tarts and cakes. Such dishes are more likely to be eaten at ·a restaurant – that favourite indulgence of many motor caravanners on holiday. And even the devotee of home-made bread is often glad to sample for a change the crusty loaves in countries where machine baking is still the exception.

A typical sink and cooker unit. It stands along the wall between dinette and
rear entrance of CI Autohomes' Wayfarer conversion of the Ford Transit.
This one has a grill and two burners, but no oven. Note how the covers
which normally conceal it have folded back to form anti-splash surfaces.
The drawer on the right is for cutlery. On the floor is the foot-pump, which
delivers water from a tank beneath the chassis.

Another reason for dispensing with the fixed oven is the existence of two substitutes. One is the collapsible oven, which folds flat. The best known, the Kubex, made of galvanized steel and weighing $5\frac{1}{2}$ lb, opens up to measure $12\frac{1}{2} \times 11\frac{1}{2} \times 9\frac{1}{2}$ in. The two shelves are removable, so that it will take any chicken or joint within these measurements. Designed to fit over a gas ring, it is in fact used by some economically minded people in their own homes for dishes not large enough to justify lighting up their main oven. The other substitute for the fixed oven is the 'Portuguese oven', a circular aluminium tube, the top half of which is removable, round a spout which fits over the gas ring. Judging by the number on sale in Portugal, it does indeed seem particularly popular there, but they can be purchased very cheaply at markets and ironmongers in all the Latin countries, although they are not always easy to find in Britain. As with everything, practice makes perfect; but I am told that once this is mastered, bread, cakes and roasts can all be turned out to consumer satisfaction. Meat and birds must, of course, be cut up to fit into the 'tube', while the bread and cakes will bake into the shape of thick wheels.

Since space is all important kitchen utensils, too, must take up as little room as possible. Ideally, saucepans should fit one inside the other, like the sets sold for camping, which generally include one or even two frying pans. These are often criticized for being too thin and liable to wear out quickly. But it is important for the motor caravanner that they should be light, since petrol consumption rises with the weight carried. Non-stick sets are particularly useful, since they are easy to clean, and therefore need less water for washing up.

A further advantage of these camping sets is that the handles are not attached. Instead, a grip handle is provided which fits any of the pans, so that they can be stacked together when not in use and take up only a corner of a cupboard. It is, of course, impracticable to hang saucepans up when the van may be driven off at any moment. Pans without handles are also less likely to be upset in a confined space, which not only makes such accidents more likely, but exacerbates their consequences.

Many camping sets include a kettle, which fits into the smallest of the saucepans. Unfortunately, these usually hold only one pint, and have a small opening and a screw-down cap. This is

fine for the camper to carry water safely, but the motor caravanner will probably prefer one with a conventional, wider lid,
and if possible with a tea-infuser, enabling it to double as a
teapot. Although the kettle of a camping set has the advantage
of a handle which folds flat, a larger 'whistling' kettle is useful,
despite the extra space it takes up. Its warning to turn out
the flame not only saves gas, but helps to prevent condensation.

Another useful piece of equipment is the pressure cooker.
Because its whole principle is to build up pressure within, so
that the cooking can be completed over a low flame, it saves on
fuel, whilst eliminating steam. It also uses far less water, speeds
up cooking time, 'reduces' tough meat in stews, and preserves the
natural juices of vegetables and other foods. With careful
observance of the makers' instructions it soon becomes a trusted
friend. Here again, a model without a long handle is to be
preferred: my own, for example, has merely a small plastic grip
on each side.

Both the pressure cooker and the Portuguese oven tend to be
used more on the Continent than in Britain; and the motor
caravanner abroad will have the opportunity of acquiring other
utensils which, unlike mere souvenirs, will give him more
pleasure to use. One is the wide shallow dish in which the
Spaniards cook paella, a rice-based mixture which properly
consists largely of shellfish, but which can be varied with
chicken and other meats. This dish is usually of metal in its home
region of Valencia, but elsewhere it is of the cheaper and more
rustic-looking glazed earthenware.

A still more useful utensil in this material is the Moroccan
tagine, a wide, saucer-like dish crowned by a separate conical
earthenware lid. Its peculiar beauty is that it cooks in two ways
at once: with the direct flame below, and with the steam forming
above inside the lid. In a sense this action is not unlike that of
the pressure cooker; and because very little steam escapes, most
of it condensing against the lid, it has similar advantages for the
motor caravanner. Connoisseurs of Moroccan cuisine, with
memories of tagines of duck with prunes and almonds, of beef
with succulent vegetables, will claim that its results taste even
better.

Tagines and paella dishes can be served straight on to the
table; and apart from formal entertaining there tends to be a

good deal of interchange in many motor caravans between what is properly kitchenware, and what is properly crockery. Here many will insist on eating off china as at home, despite its weight and the likelihood of it being smashed, whether by human error, or by the motion of the van when a plate is inadvertently left out, or a drawer is not properly secured. Others, for similar reasons, refuse to eat off plastic, although this is the lightest and cheapest of the alternatives. Many turn to the heavier and more expensive 'Melamine', which is almost indestructible, and has much of the appearance and 'feel' of conventional tableware.

The only personal view that I would put forward here is that tea *does* taste better from china, and that one or more 'proper' tea cups or mugs for guests can strikingly improve the quality of the brew.

A similar rule applies to wine, which simply does not taste the same out of anything except a glass. The answer here is to use one of the cheap, stem-less brands which can be easily replaced. Some of these, including the French 'Duralex', have a life expectancy almost as long as 'Melamine'. As regards size, it is better to err on the side of smallness, so that the same glass can serve both for wine and for aperitifs, brandy and liqueurs.

As well as cutting down on glasses, the motor caravanner would be wise to limit the number of plates to one large and one small per person, insisting that mugs should double as soup bowls, and limiting cutlery per person to one knife, one fork, one dessert spoon and one teaspoon. A few additional pieces of cutlery may be allowed for guests, but their needs in plates may be best catered for by a packet of very thin plastic dishes. Cutlery at least should be conventional in form and substance. I have tried both plastic and aluminium, and found them wanting. The cutlery drawer or container should include a sharp knife, a tin-opener, a bottle-cap lever (if not incorporated with the last named item), a corkscrew, and one of those giant sardine tin openers, which can prove very useful if the small opener provided has been lost.

There is almost everything to be said in favour of keeping a set of cooking utensils, crockery and cutlery permanently in the van, instead of raiding the kitchen at the last minute. This is not only because you will almost invariably leave something behind, but also because departure is often at short notice. It is a shame to waste part of an unexpected holiday or sunny day in unnecessary packing up. For the same reason certain basic foodstuffs are best left permanently in the van: salt, pepper, mustard, honey/jam/marmalade, tea, coffee, cocoa, powdered milk, cooking oil, rice, macaroni, biscuits (useful when bread runs out), breakfast cereals, flour and at least an 'iron ration' of tinned goods. Other 'dry goods' such as matches, soap and detergent, should also be kept. The not-so-dry goods, like butter, milk, meat and fruit can then be added at the last moment, or bought *en route*.

This brings us to the refrigerator. Many conversions now include them as a standard fitting – though rarely as part of the all-in price. There are several models available which have been specially designed for caravans. The majority of these are powered by gas, but some can also be switched over to work off the battery. The idea of this is that since the gas must be switched off when the van is moving, the refrigerator can then be kept running on the dynamo without involving any discharge. But it is all too easy to forget to switch back again when the journey is over, and five hours are all that are needed to render the battery flat.

Personal prejudice will inevitably occur in a book of this kind. It is not without value, since it is based on experience. And my own prejudice as regards refrigerators is against them. I grudge the space they occupy. I cannot sleep soundly with a pilot light burning, however automatic and foolproof the safety devices. And I thoroughly dislike the draughts which whistle through the necessary air vents on a winter's night. At such seasons, when the butter in a ventilated but enclosed cupboard is always as hard as rock, a refrigerator is superfluous. I find, in fact, that a cupboard of this type keeps fresh food in good condition during ten months of the year. For July and August it is no great hardship to buy perishable foods each day. And in July and August, it should be noted, the temperatures in southern Europe are often so high that a refrigerator designed for the English climate cannot get down to freezing point.

This is, of course, one man's preference. A majority of motor caravanners will probably want to have some form of cooling mechanism. An insulated ice-box can be kept cool by the renewal of frozen 'frost packs' or with ice blocks, which are available in many places throughout the summer.

It is a good idea to stock up on the 'iron rations' already mentioned before going abroad, since so many groceries are cheaper in Britain than elsewhere in Europe. Keep an eye open for the 'loss leader' lines in your supermarket, and compare the prices at local discount stores. If you are setting off for months rather than weeks, or perhaps for an entire winter, visit one of those warehouses which sell in bulk to personal shoppers (minimum purchases are generally a dozen tins or packets, and 7 lb bags of other goods). In theory certain countries limit the amount of foodstuffs which can be taken in to a few pounds in value, or to a few days' supply. But in practice there is a very large degree of tolerance. The Customs Officer recognizes the average motor caravanner as a valuable source of exchange, and that ample provisions of his favourite foods will enable him to extend his patronage of the host country to months rather than weeks.

Some of the things which are notably better value in Britain are tea, coffee, powdered coffee, powdered milk, butter, cheese, breakfast cereals, tinned meats, and tinned fruits. Tinned meats should always be bought as such, and not in pie form, or with vegetables added. Except in Scandinavia and the German-speaking lands vegetables can be bought cheaper abroad than in Britain, and added fresh to tinned stewing steak, ham or chicken. Although tinned fruits are cheaper here, fresh fruit is cheaper still abroad during the summer – or in Spain or Morocco all the year round – and makes for a far healthier diet. But I must leave the question of where to shop cheapest outside Britain to the sections on touring in various countries abroad.

8 Sanitation

It is the most basic of all aspects of motor caravanning life which evokes the deepest curiosity. Although inhibitions are often still strong enough to prevent its direct expression, I have been asked by an English bank manager 'Have you a lav?', and by a French count 'How do you fulfil the needs of nature?'.

Many readers will already be aware that the portable toilet has undergone great improvements in recent years. Many now offer stable bases, anti-spill lids, and self-returning bowl flaps, as well as odourless sanitary fluids, which break down the solids and paper, and prevent the formation of gases. Both Elsan and Racasan market traditional chemical toilets of this type, filled with a fluid, which in itself acts as a seal, below which the 'waste materials' disintegrate. Perdisan, Porta Potti and the Electrolux Tota-Toilet are examples of models which provide the further refinement of flushing – they are in fact 'water closets' in the fullest sense of the word. Perdisan provide a concentrated, perfumed powder as their sterilizing agent.

Capacity per 'charge', i.e. the number of times a toilet can be used without emptying, varies from 33 up to 120. In all cases the resultant effluent can be emptied down any convenient toilet. The expensive Swedish Mullbank 'biological' toilet, with a chimney to the exterior, only requires emptying twice a year; and its effluent can be used as manure.

Some owners will argue that the motor caravanner has little need of a permanent toilet. When travelling he will frequently pull up in squares or at restaurants with convenient *Hommes* and *Dames*, on sites with all facilities, or even beside well-placed hedgerows. But it must be pointed out that the motor caravanner is not travelling all the time, and that necessity can make its presence felt at some awfully inconvenient moments. Of less critical importance is the stipulation at certain less well-equipped British sites that outfits must be completely self-contained.

One way of getting the toilet outside the van is to place it in a toilet tent. Most of the ones on the market involve a certain amount of work to erect. But I have seen some home-made examples which unroll from the side of the van with a minimum of trouble. They can also serve as shower tents.

When effluent cannot be disposed of in a sewer-connected toilet, it should be buried. A small hand trowel is quite sufficient for this particular purpose; but a proper trenching tool has the advantage of being to hand for other emergencies, such as the van being stuck in sand or snow. One type widely available on the market has a retractable blade, which when folded back makes it both shorter and safer for stowing away. The plastic bags used in connection with certain 'skeleton' models of portable folding toilets should also be buried. This would seem obvious. But a manufacturer of these bags once printed them with instructions that after use they were to be tied at the neck, attached to a stone, and thrown into any convenient river or lake. Needless to say, this was before 'environment' had become one of the most frequently-used words in the language.

A trenching tool can also be useful in disposing of the rubbish from food preparation and other daily chores. More often than not, however, the motor caravanner will pass public litter bins or waste dumps as he travels. Camp sites, too, always make provision for rubbish. Those who do not wish to fit sophisticated bins and bin-linings, will find that the large paper and plastic bags given away at supermarkets in Britain and abroad make excellent free dustbins.

Personal and domestic hygiene are alike dependent on water, which must rank as high as petrol and gas in the motor caravanner's order of priorities. Without a water supply his autonomy would be destroyed, and the caravan and all its fittings become meaningless.

Several early vans stored this water and made it available for use by one of the simplest methods imaginable – gravity. A tank higher than the sink, and sometimes hidden from view within the wardrobe, released water through a tap at its lower end. Superficially straightforward, this system illustrated almost every one of the disadvantages a motor caravanner should seek to avoid in laying on his water supply.

In the first place it should not be stored high. Water is heavy. An elevated tank strains the wall to which it is attached, causes wider damage if the contents are spilled, and if large enough can even affect the vehicle's equilibrium.

In the second place it should not be difficult to fill. I remember the chore of carefully refilling, half-gallon by half-gallon, one of those elevated tanks inside my wardrobe, and even then often spilling some on my clothes in the process.

In the third place it should not be difficult to clean. It is hard to flush through a tank which is fixed and inaccessible, and if the tap is situated an inch or so above the bottom (as mine was), then that amount of water will remain permanently stagnant, and make the rest unfit for drinking.

That tap itself is the final disadvantage. For a water supply, although readily accessible, should not be instantly available. What is instantly available quickly disappears, and the carrying of water is perhaps the greatest chore the motor caravanner has to face.

A more recent and more widely-used system, pumping water up from tanks welded underneath the chassis, avoids all these disadvantages. The water lies well below the centre of gravity. It is replenished from outside the van through a filler tube with a cap like that for the petrol. Because of this resemblance it should be plainly marked 'water', possibly in several languages, and ideally should be locked to prevent it from being filled by an over-zealous pump attendant. For water, as well as fuel, can usually be replenished during visits to the forecourt. If, as is frequently the case, the tank is provided with a tap at its base, it can easily be flushed. And the very fact that water must be pumped up acts as a brake on wastage.

For this reason I look with disfavour on the electric pump, which can be switched on far too easily. Better to work for your water with the little foot or hand pumps, which are fortunately more common. Even these can fail to function, probably in some foreign land where spare parts are unobtainable; and such risks are far greater with an electric pump.

For many years now, therefore, I have deliberately reverted to the simplest system of all. I carry my water in 1 gallon plastic jerricans. As many as eight can be stored easily in a section which I have covered off at the bottom of my wardrobe. It is important that they should be protected from the light in this way; other-wise water inside clear plastic tends to colour with harmless but off-putting green algae. (Black plastic does not suffer from this disadvantage, but does not allow one to see the water level, either.)

When I have visitors, or when I intend to spend a week or more away from any water supply, I carry extra collapsible or folding containers, which double my normal water reserve. Three main types are available in camping shops. The first are collapsible 1 gallon bottles or 4 gallon containers in thin plastic. The second is the 'roll-up' carrier in an even thinner and more flexible plastic. When filled through the tap-cum-filler it swells like a huge blister to take $2\frac{1}{2}$ gallons, and can be hung up to dispense water. The third is of a similar pattern, but is made of canvas. The French graphically call it a *vache-à-l'eau*. The water is kept cool by slow evaporation through the canvas, but unless well cared for the carrier may not last many seasons.

Using jerricans not only prevents unnecessary wastage, but they also have the advantages of being easily cleaned and easily refilled. For although fixed tanks with outside access can readily be filled from hose pipes, or from service-station water dispensers, motor caravans often come to rest far from such convenient tools of civilization. To take on 15 gallons or so jug by jug is time-consuming and frustrating. Individual jerricans, on the other hand, can be filled at any hand-pump or remote spring. But they should not hold more than 1 gallon, or 5 litres, or they will be too heavy to carry.

The one considerable disadvantage of this simple system, in comparison with the underfloor tank, is that the substantial cubic space required to store the water is taken from inside the van. But even more of such valuable space is taken up when a van is fitted with the further luxury of a waste tank, in which the dirty water from the sink is accumulated until a suitable disposal point is reached. For space beneath the van is limited, and it is not easy to find room between the various projections from the chassis for both fresh- and waste-water tanks. The simplest answer to dirty-water disposal is a bucket, which can be placed beneath the waste-water pipe, or into which the plastic washbowl can be emptied in the absence of a conventional sink.

Where there is a traditional, fixed sink, this will be either of stainless steel or of perspex. Perspex is cheaper and lighter than stainless steel, but not always as easy to clean. It can also be smashed, especially if the wooden working surface, which folds down to hide the sink and kitchen unit, happens to fall suddenly when some hard object is on the draining board.

There are two good reasons for making use of a plastic bowl inside the sink. One is that, being smaller, it uses even less water than the miniature sinks installed in motor caravans. The other is that, except in the very largest vans, sinks have to double as washbasins. A separate plastic bowl is thus an invaluable aid to hygiene, enabling washing-up to be kept as an independent operation.

The built-in shower is widely regarded as the ultimate luxury in a motor caravan. The built-in bath does exist – generally on special models – but it has never caught on. Even the shortest versions are generally regarded as taking up too much space and using too much water. The built-in shower, however, takes up even more space. A bath, when all is said and done, can be used for storage when not in use. And all too frequently the means of feeding the shower are ingenious rather than practical. I recall one such arrangement whereby the sink was filled with hot water, which was then conveyed by a tube strung across the interior to a shower located in a far corner.

There is therefore much to be said in favour of the several varieties of portable shower which have been developed for campers and caravanners. These take up little space when not in use, and require only a small amount of water.

The nearest equivalent to a conventional shower operates by ejecting warm water under pressure from a thick rubber balloon. Like most of these devices it functions within a swiftly-erected, free-standing shower tent, which can be set up either inside or outside the van. One even simpler device does not require the use of a tent. This consists of a circular tube, pierced with inward-facing holes, which is placed around the neck. Water is fed up through a tube by a rubber foot-pump, which the user operates while standing in a basin of water. There is no splashing, as the gentle inward jets from the halter-tube are all caught on neck or shoulders and the water is recycled after it has run down the body. Devotees claim that this uses a mere quarter-gallon of water.

After taking a bath in a motor caravan there may well be some hot water left over, which can be used for washing clothes.

Rinsing need not be carried out at once if there is no water supply at hand, for rinsing clothes is the greatest water consumer of all. A pile of 'smalls', or a couple of men's shirts, can easily get through half a motor caravan's normal water supply. So wherever possible stockpile clothes until you stop beside a tap or a river, on a camp site, or at one of those French village communal *lavoirs*, which are specially built for the job.

The advantages of drip-dry garments will be stressed in the chapter on clothes. They wash so easily that there seems little point, even for a large family, in taking up space with a washing machine. However, Swiss, French and Japanese manufacturers have at different times produced a variety of small washing machines which are suitable for motor caravans. These consist of an aluminium globe of some 18 inches diameter with pivot and handle. The washing is placed inside, and when half-filled with warm water and detergent, it is rotated manually for a few minutes to give the same effect as an electrically-operated machine.

But the same result can be achieved with less effort, and without any such special apparatus. At the start of a journey place the clothes, water and detergent in a bucket, or large plastic container, which has a watertight seal. Leave this on its side on the floor of the van. With each stop or start, and with each bend in the road, the container will roll across the floor, with the clothes turning over. By the end of the journey they will require only rinsing.

It should also be remembered that other countries besides Britain now have conveniently sited launderettes in all towns of any size.

Drip-dry fabrics again prove their worth when the drying stage is reached. Hung up inside the van when travelling, with a window open in both the cab and the van, they will soon be dried by the current of air. The sun, of course, will do the same, and during a lunchtime halt washing can be spread out on bushes. For longer stops a clothes line with pegs should be carried. A moderately thick nylon line can serve a number of other purposes, including, in extremities, that of tow-rope.

9 Sleeping

Martin Walter hit the nail on the head when they coined the trade-mark Dormobile. For a motor caravan might well be defined as a vehicle for sleeping in. All the other functions of living could, at a pinch, be performed in other vehicles. But their whole character changes once sleeping arrangements are installed. The bed is the motor caravan's *raison d'etre*. If the bed is not a success, then the motor caravan is a failure.

In the majority of cases the bed *is* a success. I am far from being unique in sleeping better in my van than in my bed at home, let alone in some overheated, under-ventilated luxury hotel. Nor does the ability to sleep soundly seem to have much direct correlation with normal ideas of comfort. The driver's seat, which folds down to form part of a bed, usually consists of little but wires covered with imitation leather. Even so, this seems to attract Morpheus just as swiftly as the more conventional mattress of rubber or plastic foam. The man with the smallest conversion I have ever seen, a Simca 1100 saloon, in which the driver's seat wound down to give a contour like an 'N' told me that he was often tempted to sleep on this bed in the garage at home!

The most important aspect of sleeping arrangements, which seems so obvious that it tends to get overlooked, will be dealt with in Part three. It is where to park. The only point to be made here is that a sense of insecurity can in itself cause a disturbed night. Some motor caravanners can sleep soundly parked on their own in city centres, or in deep forests. Others require the assurance of human presence – a quiet village square, for example. A few, simply in order to sleep well, require the cocoon of an official camp site.

Next in importance is the mattress. Except in the case of fold-ing seats to which we have already referred, the mattress will be of rubber foam, or of the more recently developed plastic foam. I have never yet seen in a motor caravan one of the damp-absorbing interior-sprung mattresses, such as those often found in early trailer vans. Plastic foam is just as damp-resistant as rubber foam, and is lighter in weight. The thickness of a mattress is a matter of personal choice. I tend to prefer the rather firmer support of a 4 in mattress. Some, however, find this a little hard as a seat, when the full weight of the body is centred on the pelvis instead of being distributed along its length.

The type of mattress covering should also be carefully considered. Artificial leather, easily wiped down and hardwearing, is an ideal material for seats, but does not absorb the perspiration which sometimes soaks right through a sleeping bag. Textile fabrics absorb the perspiration, but also collect the dust, which so frequently invades a motor caravan in dry weather.

Whether artificial leather or a textile fabric is used, a tightly fitting sheath is to be preferred to a loose cover. The amateur can make a surprisingly professional job of this, and for textile fabrics can provide a zip-fastened opening to allow them to be removed for washing.

The fact that sitting and sleeping areas so often coincide leads on to the question of whether beds should be left permanently made up. Often, simply to provide living space, they have to be remade each day. Even where there is a possibility of choice, many prefer to do this to avoid that 'bedroomy' feeling so shunned by 'bed-sit' tenants. One way round this is to use a tight-fitting counterpane, or patterned rug.

The problem in remaking the bed each day is where to put the bedclothes when not in use. In coachbuilt models the bedding for as many as three people will not take up more than half of the luton. But in elevating-roof models sufficient bedding for two people will fill most of the under-seat storage lockers. The solution is to stuff them into fabric 'envelopes', so that they form giant cushions, often useful to sit on or lean against. If one or more of the rugs can be fitted with appropriate zips they can themselves fulfil this function.

Perhaps the greatest space-saver of all is the sleeping bag. This is not only because it rolls up into its cover, which otherwise holds a cushion in use as a pillow. It is also because it makes sheets unnecessary, and because it is so warm that fewer rugs and blankets are needed.

The amount of extra covering needed beneath and on top of a sleeping bag depends on its own filling. The down-filled bags favoured in Arctic and mountaineering expeditions are very warm indeed, and for this very reason unsuitable for the motor caravanner, who rarely has to endure such extremes. They also require dry cleaning, whereas bags filled with Terylene or Dacron can easily be washed, and on a summer's day will be dry by nightfall.

The majority of motor caravanners who travel little in the winter, are more likely to come up against extremes of heat than cold. They may for this reason be tempted to opt for lighter bags – with 26 oz rather than 38 oz Terylene filling, for example. Again this is a matter for individual choice. I prefer a 'heavy' covering, and find that by undoing a foot or two of zip I can still keep cool on a hot night. A more important point is that heavier-filled sleeping bags tend to be of better quality in other respects too. Their greater initial expense is offset not only by increased durability, but also by such hidden but important bonuses as a full overlap to cover the zip on the inside.

A new type of sleeping bag, developed for use by astronauts, folds up to a mere third of the normal size. There are also super-efficient 'space blankets', which have similar advantages. These work by reflecting back 90% of the covered person's body heat from a thin aluminium panel, which can, however, lead to problems of condensation.

Condensation is even more of a drawback with inflatable pillows. Although these can be packed away so easily, it is better to have a few scattered cushions, which can be slipped into pillow cases at night, and which give the van a homely air by day. Even spare underwear and woollies packed into a pillow slip are preferable to the greasy feel of a hot cheek against damp rubber.

What should be the dimensions of the beds, and where should they be situated? As regards width, a single bed should be at least 2 ft wide, and a double bed no less than 3 ft 6 in. Given that a bed should be at least 6 ft long – though I know motor cara-vanners of 5 ft 10 in who claim to be comfortable curling up in a length of only 5 ft 8 in – the position depends largely upon the basic vehicle. If this is 6 ft across, then the bed can extend trans-versely across its width; if less, it must run down the side.

Positioning the beds transversely economizes on space, and leaves a larger area free for other activities when the beds are made up. If the bed is not at the rear of the van, it also means that the sleeper is not lying against an outside wall. However good the insulation, it is surprising what rheumatic pains can develop when one lies against an exterior wall exposed to a bitter winter wind.

Transverse beds also have the advantage of being beneath full-sized windows, thus facilitating one of the greatest pleasures of the motor caravanner: reading in bed. This can also be enjoyed by occupants of the rear-end beds in conversions of such vans as the VW and the Fiat 903 cc, with side door and large back window. The Cotswold, a coachbuilt conversion, with side entrance, is equally well lit, and one of its advantages is that sitting and sleeping areas are situated as far as possible away from driving cab and engine.

Any van slept in by more than three people is bound to have some of its beds situated away from the main body of the van. Sometimes the driver's and passenger's seats convert into one transversal or into two longitudinal beds, thus making use of what is so often the 'wasted space' of the cab. A transverse bed in this situation is all too often on the short side, and only suitable for children. Both types of bed may be exposed to draughts from badly fitting doors, or to the heat which builds up in the metal-work of cabs in summer.

Heat can also be a problem for overhead bunks, and for those 'upstairs' double beds, which in certain recent coachbuilt conversions have replaced the luton above the cab. In this case the offender is convected heat rising upwards. Although this can make sleep difficult if there is no window or skylight, the warmth will be welcomed when winter chills penetrate the easily folded, but all too thin nylon cloth, which now forms the material of many hammock-type upper bunks. Again, it is wise to have as many bedclothes beneath as on top, but brown paper will help prevent the cold striking upwards.

Two important aspects of motor caravan sleeping arrange-ments – their versatility, and their under-bed storage lockers – can often be in conflict. The bed which becomes a 'dinette' when its central section is raised to form a table, loses at least a third of its locker space in the process. The ready-made bed, which when not in use folds up bodily on a hinge against the wall, is ideal in trailer caravans, where considerations of weight impose a limit on the amount which can be carried. But in a

A dinette arranged for sitting, on a Bedford converted by Auto-Sleepers. Note how the working area is concentrated in the foreground.

The same dinette arranged for sleeping. A table has been lowered between the seats, and the back-rest cushions re-positioned to form a double bed.

motor caravan it spells wasted storage space, and I have not seen one included in any model since the earliest Roadrangers. However, there have been two interesting solutions, which in some respects had the best of both worlds.

One was an early Danbury, the Multicar, whose furniture was made up of a number of interchangeable 'modules'. One contained the 'kitchen', one the 'bathroom', while two identical empty chests were available for clothes, tinned supplies, and so on. They could be shifted about to form various bed patterns, sleeping four adults and one child, or two adults and four children, or they could be placed one on top of another to provide extra living space by day.

The second was the Clavercar Estate (now discontinued), an elevating-roof model, in which the kitchen and wardrobe unit alone was fixed. The seats not only combined to make two double beds, or one double and two singles, but could seat up to ten passengers. They could even be taken outside along with the table for an alfresco meal, or to furnish a frame tent or awning. Yet their simple hinged tubular supports left all the space underneath for storage, including a big removable wooden trunk, which formed part of the Clavercar's fittings.

10 Clothes

The simpler the motor caravanner's clothes, and the fewer taken, the more comfortable he or she will be. How many times has a passenger of mine, packing up unused shoes, woollens and suits at the end of a long trip, exclaimed: 'Why ever did I bring all these? All that I've actually needed are the jeans and pullover I'm wearing, with the swimsuit underneath'.

I can always find sympathy for them, despite their having unnecessarily cluttered up my cupboards. For it is only by experience that I have at last reduced my own motor caravanning wardrobe to the bare essentials. Where I do have reason to complain is when, despite my earnest entreaties, they insist on bringing these clothes in vast suitcases.

For a suitcase is a nuisance in a motor caravan. A soft-sided hand-grip, or an ex-military kitbag is useful for emergencies, and will roll up to almost nothing. Cardboard cartons can be thrown away once their contents are emptied, and as easily replaced when needed again at departure.

The same considerations of space-saving and of convenience should determine the choice of the clothes themselves. The advantages of drip-dry fabrics cannot be too highly stressed. It hardly needs saying that a motor caravanner welcomes their swift-drying and non-ironing qualities even more than the normal householder. But their crease-resistance, enabling them to be folded tight and stored in small or narrow cupboards, which would crumple cotton or linen, is equally important. Indeed, their adoption even for such formal wear as women's dresses, or men's suits, trousers and jackets, means that the hanging wardrobe can be dispensed with altogether. Not that formal wear is a major, or even an important part of motor caravanners' clothing. They are at leisure, and should therefore dress with a view first to their own comfort.

11 Accessories

Accessories can, of course, include anything from plastic flowers to kennels. Neither one of these is unknown in a motor caravan. But the only two types we shall discuss here are the two that most readers will wish to have: open-air furniture, and that which, for want of a better term, we shall define as electronic entertainment.

Anyone owning a motor caravan will already have certain pieces of open-air furniture. A free-standing table is as useful outside the van as inside (but be ready for a Formica surface to crinkle up at the edges under a hot sun). Occasionally chairs, including the driver's and the front passenger's, are removable. One or two conversions – an early Danbury, and more recently the ingenious Clavercar – have been deliberately designed to allow their free-standing seats, as well as their table, to be moved outside at a moment's notice.

Several other articles in the van can also play a double role. Seat squabs are more comfortable than cushions for sitting on with your back up against the van or a tree. Seated at this level the step, where it is not incorporated with the van, is just at the right height to serve as a picnic table. Whole mattresses can be pulled out for sunbathing. Those who, like myself, prefer a plastic bowl to a sink, and a single gas bottle with burner to a static cooker, can in seconds transfer their cooking and washing up out of doors.

However, there is plenty of special equipment available. Folding chairs are the most obvious choice. I would advise chairs rather than stools, which although less bulky are not worth even that small amount of space. It is more comfortable to sprawl on the ground than to sit for long periods without a back rest. I would also recommend chairs which fold side to side (from the user's point of view), rather than back to front. For if the supporting bar comes under the thighs it can impede circulation and make prolonged relaxation uncomfortable.

There are points for and against both cotton and nylon as

seat covering. Nylon is more durable, does not absorb damp, and can simply be wiped dry after a rainstorm. But it has a 'slippery' feel, which not everyone finds comfortable. Cotton takes a little time to dry, and wears out quicker, but costs only a few pence and a few stitches to replace.

The classic folding camp chair has three disadvantages for motor caravan use. It is of an awkward shape, which is too large even when folded to fit conveniently into a locker or wardrobe. Because of its steel frame it is relatively heavy, and for the same reason it is liable to rust. The 'Gadabout' chair has been designed as the answer to all these problems. Made of aluminium, and covered in a tough nylon, it is rustproof, weighs only a couple of pounds and has a crossed-legs pattern, which enables it to fold up to the size of a thick walking-stick. Inevitably it costs up to three times the price of an ordinary folding chair, but many consider this a well-justified expense.

As much or more can be spent on the various tubular folding armchairs and chaises-longues on the market. Their extra bulk gives them the disadvantages of the classic folding chair to an advanced degree; but I know efficient and otherwise practical motor caravanners who find them worth the space and inconvenience.

Inflatable furniture provides another alternative. The range includes straightforward air mattresses, mattresses divided into three 'biscuits', which fold to make a low chair, and complete upholstered armchairs, some of which can be converted to ordinary airbeds. The Sumatra boat which will be described in Chapter 12, also forms a most comfortable lounger. All have the advantage of packing neatly into any available corner.

Cooking outside offers an opportunity to get away from con-ventional caravan food to dishes which involve rather more mess and smell. A small collapsible barbecue in heavy-gauge steel, and with folding legs, will probably take up a little more room than the frying pan, but can be stowed deep in the recesses of a storage locker when not in use. Another useful device is the Swedish Akker smoker, which is particularly suited to that trickiest of caravan foods – fish. It folds into a box smaller than a medium-sized dictionary.

'Electronic entertainment' can also be enjoyed in the open air, though it should be turned well down. But it is above all inside the van that it is most appreciated. Some of the happiest motor caravanning memories are of listening to the radio news over breakfast in bed; hearing good music while doing the chores; getting accustomed to the sound of a foreign language over a leisurely lunch; listening to the clear tones of the BBC's General Overseas Service in some far-off foreign land; and, perhaps best of all, switching on some favourite programme as one snuggles down into a sleeping bag on a cold winter's night.

Electronic entertainment for the motor caravanner is first and foremost the radio. Any small portable set with medium- and long-wave reception is, of course, sufficient for listening to the BBC and to local stations in Britain. But for anyone going abroad, or for anyone in England wishing to hear concerts from the Continent, a set offering short-wave reception is essential.

Unfortunately most English and Japanese manufacturers produce little between the very costly 'round the world' monsters, and small portables with one or two short-wave selectors without sufficient 'bandspread' to secure clear definition. Manufacturers who produce very good sets with several short-wave bands include the British Radiomobile, the Japanese Sharp, the German Blue Spot (Blau Punkt), and the Dutch Philips with its British subsidiary. The slim, graceful models of the last are backed up by a particularly strong world-wide chain of agents.

It is the lack of this readily available repair service which is the one disadvantage of the Russian transistor sets. In every other respect they are the motor caravanner's dream, for their eight wavebands (long, medium, and six short) provide such detailed coverage that a special 'bandspread' tuner is not necessary. The larger models not only give excellent reception, but they have the advantage of using eight $1\frac{1}{2}$ volt batteries which add up to 12 volts. This means that they can be run directly off the engine battery (except on the Renault 4L, which has 6 volt batteries). The smaller sets, with six $1\frac{1}{2}$ volt batteries (9 volts), require a small transformer.

It is well worth including a stock of radio batteries with your supplies if the journey is to be longer than three months. (Even with frequent use a new set of batteries will last at least that length of time). For there are very few places – though Ceuta, Melilla and the Canaries are amongst them – where they are cheaper than in Britain. This supply should include batteries for any cassette players or tape recorders, which use them up more quickly. It is worth remembering when buying battery-operated equipment, and this includes torches, that if they all use the same type of battery then you will only have to buy one interchangeable size. Even a battery which is too weak to turn the tape-recorder may yet have sufficient 'juice' to provide many hours of radio listening.

Good radio reception in a motor caravan depends, however, not only on the model chosen and on the batteries. Radio waves have great difficulty in penetrating the steel shell of a commercial conversion, and even the aluminium shell of many coachbuilt conversions. The 'pull-out' aerials incorporated in most models are not really long enough, and do not in any case extend outside the van. But there is no need to go to great expense in fitting an outside aerial. Any suitable length of insulated wire can be fitted to a suitable socket, and either wound round the roof, or attached to a suitable pole or tree if one is going to park for any length of time. In coachbuilt vans where the 'luton' above the cab is in fibreglass, the aerial can be draped *inside* this.

What to listen to when this apparatus is set up? The *Radio Times* only gives the briefest selection of Continental programmes, and it may not always be convenient to get the information from newspapers abroad. The best sources are the various broadcasting authorities themselves, who, when all is said and done, depend on listeners as their *raison d'être*. So here are some addresses:

Radio France, 116 avenue du Président Kennedy, Paris 16ᵉ, France.

R.A.I., Direzione dei Servizi delle Trasmissioni per l'Estero, viale Mazzini 14, 00195-Roma, Italy.

Radio Nacional de España, General Yagüe 1, Madrid 20, Spain. Radiotelevisione Italiana (RAI) are particularly helpful. Their illustrated brochures, available in several languages including English, are produced with real Italian style. And the most useful and helpful of all, and still the most listened-to, more than thirty years after it sustained Nazi-occupied Europe, is the BBC General Overseas Service, whose address is: Bush House, PO Box 76, Strand, London WC2 B4PH.

Television sets in motor caravans are by no means out of the question since the introduction of the smaller Japanese models.

Care should be taken to purchase one capable of receiving 625 line transmissions if it is to be used abroad. Here, even more than in the case of a radio, there is everything to be said in favour of a model, such as the Commando, which can run not only off mains and batteries, but also off a 12 volt car battery.

Anyone who contemplates installing television would certainly regard the cassette player or tape recorder as worth the extra amount of space taken up. Tuning in to the excellent music programmes of the British, French, Italian and Portuguese Broadcasting Corporations will at most times of the day yield some pleasing concerto or sonata. But a tape recorder or cassette player will enable you to choose your own music, and will give you higher quality reproduction. Cassette players such as those manufactured by Radiomobile and Philips, have separate speakers which can be connected to provide optimum stereo effect, and which can be sunk into the panelling, or even into cupboard doors, so as to take up the minimum of space. One of the advantages of cassette players for motor caravanners is the fact that cassettes take up so little room; a small library of them will only occupy the same length on a shelf as a single thick book.

12 Annexes

For the purposes of this chapter an annexe can be defined as anything which provides extra living space. The most common type of annexe on trailer vans is the awning, but this is a less useful piece of equipment for the motor caravanner. For although it provides an extra room, and its neat, watertight flange fits on to the side of the van, it becomes, for these very reasons, a major operation to detach it when you want to drive away. And once detached it collapses, for the side of the van is its main support.

Most annexe tents designed specially for motor caravans, therefore, are really frame tents with a somewhat awkward 'sleeve' which fits over the back of the vehicle. Hence they are free standing when the sleeve is removed, and can be left to reserve a plot on a site, and to store the equipment not required on a day's excursion. Many users find them invaluable, although their appearance is less than pleasing.

Purchasers should note that an annexe designed for a fixed or elevating-roof van will not necessarily fit a coachbuilt model, and certainly not one with a side door. Also, that depreciation on tents of all kinds is very rapid indeed, so a used annexe might as well be sold by including it in the price asked for the van.

One admirable device, midway between an awning and an annexe, unfolds directly from the gutter, where it is kept rolled up when not in use. This means that it does not take up space either inside or on a roof rack, making it ideal for the mini-motor caravans and estate-car conversions, where extra space really is a necessity when they are used by more than one person.

Where more room than this is required, however, there is much to be said in favour of a separate tent, standing quite independently alongside the van. Free-standing tents are available in every size from the one-man, one-pole bivouac, weighing less than 5 lb, to complete canvas bungalows weighing over 100 lb, and measuring 15 or more feet square when erected. The price of the latter runs well into three figures. But because they take a little trouble to put up, and occupy more space in the boot than some families anticipate, they can often be acquired very cheaply, second-hand but almost new, from disappointed purchasers. Try the classified columns of local newspapers, and *Exchange and Mart*.

On the fixed-roof conversions which do not have room for bunks, extra space is essential when used by more than two people. A little-known answer to this dilemma is the roof-tent. This provides a ready-made 'first floor', smaller than a frame tent but with the comfort of a solid floor, and opening up to reveal a ready-made bed. For some reason these have never really caught on, although they would be even more useful to the car owner who did not wish to go to the expense of buying a trailer caravan for his summer holidays.

The earliest type, which is now again in production as the 'Air Camper' by A. J. C. Trailers, Houghton Regis, Dunstable, Bedfordshire, opened like a pram hood to form a tent 7 ft × 4 ft, but only $3\frac{1}{2}$ ft high. It is thus unsuitable for anything except sleeping, and has little space when folded to store anything except the bedclothes and the rather thin mattress. However, a useful little awning can be hung from the half of the roof which opens out.

The tent trailer provides an alternative to the free-standing or roof-tent. The smallest of these are little more than bivouacs on wheels. The largest provide two full-size double beds on either side of a wide kitchen/living area, which can be further multiplied by awnings. The trailers not only provide somewhere to stow the tent, but also somewhere to stow much else besides. In some models the lid, which opens to form part of the solid floor, is equipped with rails and luggage platforms to act as a ready-made roof rack. Their weight and wind resistance are so low that they make little difference to performance and consumption. For the smaller van carrying a large family they would seem to have much to offer.

Yet they have their critics, who dismiss them as combining the disadvantages of both tents and caravans. Certainly they take a little time to erect. Despite their solid floors they are not insulated, and offer the same discomforts as living under canvas beneath a hot sun or during a cold night. Like trailer caravans, too, they require towbars and wiring for lights; they have their support legs to be wound down at each arrival, and up at each departure; and they involve travelling on six wheels instead of merely four.

So why not tow a complete caravan while one is about it? There are in fact quite a number of motor caravans which do just that. With a fanfare of publicity Caravans International have more than once handed over a special order of Highwayman with Sprite Alpine, or Autohome with Musketeer. The idea appealed to me very much during my early years of motor caravanning. I liked the concept of total autonomy, of concentrating all cooking arrangements in either one vehicle or the other, of being able to offer a higher standard of comfort to my guests – and, perhaps most of all, the possibility of getting right away from them whenever I wanted.

The years have dulled this yearning. Experience has taught me that a motor caravan, and especially a coachbuilt one, can provide all the permanent space required by the individual or the smaller family. Towing a caravan means that you not only double your ferry charges, but you surrender mobility, and the ability to park anywhere and everywhere, to camp wild. In short, you are denying the very essence of motor caravanning, in sacrificing precisely those freedoms which a motor caravan alone can give.

It is surprising how infrequently even a tent or awning is needed to supplement a well-equipped motor caravan. A few folding chairs placed in the shade of the van can be moved out of the sun as the shadows swing round. A gas bottle with burner attachment and windshield can be used for cooking outside. On warm nights the long cable of a fluorescent lamp can bring light from the battery. And with these half dozen accessories swiftly packed away, you are all set to move on to pastures new.

13 Auxiliary transport

There was once a special conversion of a bus, which had separate lounge, separate kitchen, separate bathroom with running hot water, separate bedrooms, and a central heating system. And this was not all. When the tailgate opened down to form a ramp, out from its 'garage' came a bubble car.

The proud owner no doubt found it invaluable for travelling on narrow or otherwise unsuitable roads, or to places where it would be hard to park, and also simply for saving petrol. For these same three reasons many owners of smaller and less luxurious motor caravans provide themselves with proportionately smaller and less luxurious forms of auxiliary transport.

Inevitably this must be two-wheeled. There are four main choices: folding bicycles, bicycles, mopeds, and miniature motorcycles.

At first sight a folding bicycle seems the obvious answer. It can be packed away in the luton, or lifted just inside the door at the moment of departure. It is ready in seconds for the run to the farm down the road for milk, or to the Poste Restante for mail. Certain models have extensible seat and handlebars, enabling them to be used by any member of the family.

For anything longer than a ride into the village, or down to the beach, a straightforward touring bicycle is more suitable. It offers good exercise. It can take you through a crowded city at a faster pace than the jam-packed lines of traffic, and even someone out of training will have little difficulty in covering twenty or thirty miles on one.

However for the lone motor caravanner, wandering slowly round Europe for months on end, thirty miles, giving a radius of a mere fifteen, just is not far enough. And at eight or ten miles an hour it is not fast enough either. He soon realizes that with a little power, to enable him to cover all his side-excursions on two wheels, he could cut the annual mileage of his motor caravan by a third or more. He could almost wipe out his ferry charges by

These British motor caravanners holidaying in Holland are finding their bicycles an invaluable form of auxiliary transport.

taking a moped with bivouac tent instead of the van to Elba and Corsica and the Balearics, and perhaps even to England if he is only returning there for a week or two.

There are numerous mopeds on the market: British, French, Italian and Japanese. Honda produce a good model with a four-stroke engine, but on most other makes the engines are two-stroke, using a mixture of oil with petrol (generally in a proportion of about 4%, though each maker has his own recommendation).

The simplest and cheapest, but also the slowest, is the Velosolex, an upright, solid-looking bicycle with rather thick tyres, whose tiny 49 cc engine below the handlebars turns the front wheel round by friction on the tyre. My own has saved me hundreds of pounds in petrol and ferry charges, for its consumption is nearly 200 miles per gallon, and spare parts are very cheap. Its insurance in France automatically includes a Green Card for use in England and the usual West European countries, as well as Tunisia and Morocco, which can be expensive extras for anyone insuring with a British company. But then no British company will permanently insure a moped abroad in any case – they claim that it is not worth the paper work.

There exist at least three mopeds, Velosolex now included, which fold or split into two parts for storage. But they are relatively expensive; and specialists assure me that they would not stand up to really hard wear.

So some motor caravanners might consider one of the miniature motorcycles which are available. These are generally low-slung, with small wheels and fat little tyres, and often with extensible seat and handlebars, which drop down for packing away. But again they are far from cheap, and although they are useful for short trips, I have yet to meet anyone using one on any serious or extended journey.

The most obvious place to park a normal-sized and non-folding bicycle or moped would seem to be either the front or the back of the motor caravan. Over the years I have observed a number of such arrangements, with the cycles strapped to some form of projecting support. But I have always seen them abroad, and always on vehicles from some other country (for example on American vans in France). The legal requirements would have to be carefully checked with the police before any such support were fitted in Britain. It would certainly be specified that no other road user would be placed in any danger, that no lights were obscured, and that anything projecting beyond the line of the lights was itself lighted. A little consideration will reveal how difficult it might prove to carry out even these elementary precautions. And the nuisance of removing a cycle every time you wanted to open the back door hardly needs elaboration.

The alternative is to store the cycle bodily inside the van. The inconvenience is less than might be supposed. Once the van is parked the bicycle or moped can be left outside and locked up with padlock and chain. It is then ready when needed, but does not clutter up the interior. For this it is important that the machine should be cheap: at once undesirable to a thief, and of little loss if stolen. This is one reason why I would stress the advantages of a second-hand Velosolex, rather than those of folding mopeds or miniature motorcycles bought new.

Whilst on the subject of auxiliary transport, we must remember that not all locomotion is by road. It may be many years before a bubble helicopter can be strapped to the roof, or a pair of wings hung up in the wardrobe. But how often have you drawn up beside a lake or river bank, and wished that you had a canoe or punt, in which to glide away. For the motor caravanner this dream can be realized. He has the choice of three types of boat: rigid, folding, and inflatable.

Under the heading of rigid come canoes and dinghies. The light insubmergible dinghies of double-skin polythene are ideal for motor caravan use. The French Sportyak, for example, weighs only 42 lb, yet it will safely carry up to three adults. It requires no upkeep or painting, and its two-tone colour scheme always looks fresh. It can only be carried on the roof, and therefore would only be suitable for a commercial fixed-top conversion.

In view of the lack of space in such conversions, and the amount of room occupied by a rigid boat, thought has often been given to the possibility of using a boat to provide extra living space. One ingenious solution, which appeared in 1964, was the Car-a-boot. This was a Mini van with a removable lid-less box on its roof, on top of which a glass-fibre dinghy fitted upside down, providing shelter for a double bed. A small caravan extension (*not* a trailer), was attached to the back, making a six-wheeled vehicle. The idea of the boat-and-bed on the roof, but without the caravan attachment, has always seemed eminently practicable to me.

Perhaps one day someone will develop a 'high-top' motor caravan similar to a certain trailer caravan, which has a 12 ft boat fitting like a glove over its stream-lined, keel-like roof.

Folding boats take up very much less space than the rigid varieties and there are considerable differences between one make and another. The type which collapses lengthwise, from a width of approximately 3 ft down to 7 in, or even $2\frac{1}{2}$ in, will still measure the same length and depth. But to stow even a short 8 ft boat inside a van will be the greatest nuisance; while a reasonably-sized boat of 14 ft, however narrow when folded, will barely fit inside the largest coachbuilt models. The only solution is to place the boat on some form of roof rack, or to take it only on journeys where it will definitely be used.

Twenty minutes, on the other hand, is the time given by the manufacturers for the assembly of a different type of folding boat. This is a canoe consisting of a framework of carefully-built sections of seasoned wood with brass fittings, which folds into one bag, and of a one-piece hull of heavy-duty rubberized fabric, which folds into another. These boats range in weight from 30 lb to 100 lb, depending on whether they seat one, two, three, or four persons, and whether mast and sails are included to fit them for sailing.

They are practically uncapsizable, and with the addition of inflatable buoyancy chambers completely unsinkable, and are as streamlined and as tough as rigid canoes, but are lighter in weight. Their carrying capacity varies from 300 lb to as much as 1,200 lb, so that a very considerable amount of equipment can be stowed in the ample, weather-protected spaces under the fore and aft decking. This makes them particularly suitable for long-distance waterway tours. The best-known make, the Granta of Cambridge, has been used in such widely different waters as the Loire, African swamps, and the Atlantic off St Helena.

Unfortunately, this type takes as long to put away as to erect, and is therefore best suited to the motor caravanner who intends to spend days at a time beside water. This also applies to the third type, the inflatable boat. This can be blown up easily enough with a foot pump, or better still, with a 12 volt air pump, which can also be used to suck the air out, so that the boat can be folded away into its sack. The rubberized canvas must be both clean and dry before it is folded, and if it has been in the sea it must be washed with fresh water to prevent the salt from rotting the fabric. I found that this operation took a long hour with my own French 12 ft inflatable canoe, with the result that I used it less and less.

Yet the motor caravanner likes to feel that he can take to the water if he really wishes. For this reason I carry a delightful device called a Sumatra boat, best described as an extended air mattress, which inflates to form a miniature catamaran. Because of its simple form it can be folded up quickly into a very small space. It serves too as a comfortable seat out of doors, and as a spare bed in emergencies.

On the rare occasions when I do take to the water, I use the paddles of my old canoe, although they are really too big for the job. I so much enjoy the expression on visitors' faces when they suddenly spy them, strapped to the ceiling on either side of the roof vent. 'Whatever are those oars for? You don't mean to say that a motor caravan can actually carry a boat, too?'

14 Keeping out of trouble
by John Hunt

Trouble with the vehicle worries motor caravanners like any other road users. As a driver you will already have decided what provision is advisable for ordinary motoring: whether to belong to a motoring organization or a vehicle-recovery service – or both. So I shall concentrate my remarks on more ambitious travelling.

The difference between Henry Myhill and myself – both dedicated motor caravanners – is that he takes his holidays in a house whilst I go motor caravanning. Conversely, he *lives* in a motor caravan, I live at home.

If you intend to become a Henry Myhill, your approach will be different from that of a John Hunt. The latter, when he travels abroad, will stock up with every conceivable kind of emergency provision for motor car and caravan *and* body and mind. A Henry will have learnt to live off the country he happens to be in and will have no more emergency equipment than would an average nomad away for a week or two in Britain.

Inexperienced nomads should take too much rather than too little. On encountering some others abroad, I have been amazed at their lack of forethought. It seems to be asking for trouble to travel without aspirins or a tummy settler, a spare gas mantle or fluorescent tube, a roll of insulating tape or a hose bandage.

Of course, you're not going to the North Pole or darkest Africa and most western countries are at least as civilized as we are in the UK. But things are different and obtaining what's needed in an emergency in a foreign country will be more difficult for the uninitiated.

Survival . . . under difficulties is an attitude of mind
Emergencies have a habit of happening at inconvenient times and places. But wherever you are, your motor caravan is your home and even if it breaks down and cannot be moved, it can be lived in, if properly provisioned, until help arrives. So,

before you think about how you are going to get out of trouble, are you prepared to cope with it?

The chances are ten to one that there will be food aboard. Many nomads keep an 'iron rations' box which lives always in the van. It will contain non-perishable items such as tinned soup and fruit and probably dried vegetables. At infrequent intervals the contents are eaten – but they should be replaced before they are consumed.

The same applies to the medical and first-aid box. When the aspirins, cough mixtures and so on have been in the van for some months, they should be taken into the household stock and immediately replaced. Bandages can be kept for years but plasters and antiseptics do need periodical renewal.

If the vehicle breaks down in an isolated place, at least you can live in it for the time being. (If it becomes a traffic hazard, it's in the way of things, and help will arrive before you've had time to put the kettle on! There's a moral there somewhere.) Have you, as well as food, sufficient water on board? Some motor caravanners like to reduce weight by travelling with empty water containers. By all means change to fresh water when the destination is reached, but do travel with a reasonable amount of the precious liquid. A couple of gallons would keep a family going for a day or more – provided nobody washed.

Increasingly, motor caravans are equipped with built-in water tanks which should, of course, be filled. The water can be kept sweet by the use of a charcoal type filter on the outlet – don't forget the spare cartridge.

Insurance

A few extra-cautious motor caravanners carry a picnic stove and small tent. Then, if the van is involved in an accident or develops a mechanical failure and has to go for repair, at least there is somewhere to live for a few days. Such an unhappy eventuality can, however, be covered by insurance which will pay for alternative transport and/or hotel charges. But will it give you cash on the spot?

Some nomads rely on vouchers supplied by a motoring organization. My own experience is that they are virtually worthless. I have not found a garage willing to accept them and finally gave up the idea of relying on them when the British

Airways clerk at an international airport in Germany refused to accept them for an emergency flight home. You need money – not vouchers.

The bank account is no longer the prerogative of the monied classes and you should carry your cheque book and cheque card. You will then be able to draw cash in the currency of the country you happen to be in – and at almost any bank. I don't suggest that you should run your account into the red, although you might decide to do so if the need were urgent and make apologetic noises to your bank manager on returning home. It would be more diplomatic to arrange a temporary overdraft in case of dire necessity before leaving for the holiday.

Credit cards are becomingly increasingly acceptable in Europe and already some garages will accept them just as they do at home.

There are other methods of insurance. The Caravan Club, for example, will cable money to a member in distress. This is a loan, which must be repaid. Europ Assistance (apply direct or through the RAC or Camping Club) have a flying ambulance and a permanently manned telephone number in London. Their instructions are to ring if trouble strikes and wait for the help which will be sent via one of their overseas agents. The motoring organizations offer telephones manned around the clock, and sometimes there are offices abroad too.

Recovery

I once met a couple who had actually been rescued and towed to the ferry by a real English AA man in Belgium. They were met by the AA at Dover, too. But I have also seen a motor caravan 'recovered' by the AA from Germany. The operation took weeks and the van was vandalized when delivered.

Many of the clubs offer vehicle-recovery service. No doubt the system works efficiently most of the time. It's the failures that receive publicity. When my van developed a leaking petrol tank in Europe we thought the affiliation of our motoring organization to its foreign equivalent would result in the standard of helpfulness we could expect in England. Not a bit of it. We were told to go to a nearby garage and see if they could help. They couldn't – or wouldn't. Nor would the next half dozen, but eventually we found one willing to take the van in. The mechanic worked on it all day (a replacement tank was unobtainable) and then said there was no charge! It's all a matter of luck.

Relais Routiers offer a different sort of succour. It's the organization for French lorry drivers. The idea is that if a member sees you stranded by the roadside he'll stop and, if he can't get you going, will tow you to the nearest garage. We've halted in many laybys in France but have never been offered help, even when checking water and oil levels under the bonnet. Perhaps we just didn't look distressed.

And this is what you've got to do, if you really do need road-side help. Don't be afraid of making an exhibition of yourself. Bring the family into the act too. You've got to wring the heart-strings of passing motorists. It will be more effective if the male adult can remain hidden (brewing the tea, for instance) whilst wife and youngsters ferret around despairingly in the engine compartment – but in full view of anyone who might show interest.

Obtaining help, wherever it may be, is easier for the extrovert. So often it's necessary to make a fuss before others will react. If you really do need a doctor or an ambulance, you're more likely to succeed if you're doubled up with pain, preferably lying on path or roadway. (Don't try this in India; passers-by will just step over you.) If you need help, but not desperately, just make a nuisance of yourself and don't be put off with an initial refusal. If, like me, you're of a retiring disposition, you'll just have to grit your teeth and go on trying. Success comes at last to the persevering.

Spares and remedies

You can hire a spares kit from your motoring organization. Personally, I borrow a few items from my local garage. They know the vehicle and its likely failings. The same applies to the human body. The owner knows its short-comings and should stock up with such items as spare spectacles, tummy pills, sunburn lotion, hot-water bottles as necessary.

It would be wasting space (and increasing the price of this book) to duplicate the valuable first-aid hints and remedies for both vehicles and humans published in handbooks of motoring organizations, so I'll conclude the chapter with a few highly personalized suggestions.

What do I do when:

'Continental tummy' strikes? You'll be glad you brought a portable loo and your favourite remedy. If you haven't, visit a chemist or doctor with phrase book and bulging wallet. Keep receipts so you can claim on insurance on return. Tummy troubles can be caused by excitement. A sedative may help. Avoid very cold drinks. Eat only fresh or well-cooked bland food. Wash and sterilize salads. Boil milk. Pass all drinking water through your filter.

Someone can't stand the heat? Drink plenty of water (you'll be glad of the filter on the water tap) and take more salt. Take anti-sunburn tablets if necessary. If you have no awning or sun umbrella, make shady lean-to with blanket tied to side of van, saturated with water if necessary.

Someone is really ill? Hope there's a reciprocal health agreement and visit doctor, then chemist, or hospital with the form E111, which you obtained from the local Health and Social Security Office before leaving home. Sometimes you'll have to pay a proportion or the full cost and claim later. Procedures vary in countries within the EEC. Always advisable to have medical insurance too – essential if self-employed.

Our vehicle is involved in an accident? Use warning triangle which you have brought. Procedures vary. As a general rule, don't move the vehicle, especially if someone is hurt. Render first aid, of course, but don't forget to take measurements and fill in accident report (probably in duplicate) supplied by your insurance company or motoring organization. Take photographs if possible. Make sure approaching traffic is warned. Read up correct procedures for the country in your club's overseas handbook. Above all, don't admit liability. In Spain, be glad of bail bond.

Our vehicle breaks down? Don't panic. Laugh if you can. Get out of danger if possible. Use warning triangle. Relax (light pipe, or cigarette, put kettle on) and think things through. Study faults list in handbook. Can you cure trouble yourself? If not, put on 'desperation act' (see above) and even hold out your tow rope expectantly.

A tyre is punctured? Procedure as for breakdowns. Be thankful that you rehearsed wheel changing at home. If wheel in cradle under van, use jack under cradle to take weight rather than risk wrenched muscles. If too low, use your levelling ramps. When you have puncture repaired, you may be glad that you bought a spare inner tube of the correct size – even if tyres are tubeless.

The engine begins overheating? Be gentle with throttle. Move down one gear and keep revs fairly high. Turn on heater and booster fan if necessary. If water lost from radiator, wait till engine cools before topping up – or top up with hot water from kettle. Next time you buy petrol, make sure you get 'super'. If hose has burst, use hose bandage which you bought from accessory shop before leaving home.

The petrol tank leaks? Provided it is not wafer thin with rust, patch it with one of those substances like putty sold by stationers for sticking pictures on to walls. Remember it is only a temporary repair. I'm told silencer bandage works, too, if it can be tied in place.

The camp sites are full? Depends on the country. Some allow use of town carparks, others rest areas on motorways. If desperate, pull on to verge or layby and move on if asked/told to do so.

The site owner overcharges? Point to scale of charges which should be displayed. If no satisfaction, keep receipts and take up with club or foreign tourist office on return home. (Don't expect all charges to be as quoted in the site book, which was probably printed six or nine months ago.)

The caravan catches fire? Get everyone out. Remind yourself that all fires begin with little flames. Turn gas off at cylinder. Use fire extinguisher, water in waste bucket – anything. Don't panic but make lots of noise to attract help – especially at night. This is one occasion when assistance will probably be immediately forthcoming. Send someone to site office to sound alarm/ telephone fire brigade.

I lose my money/passport? Go to police. They're used to it. If money or travellers' cheques, come away with proof that loss has been reported; otherwise your insurance company may doubt you.

I spend all my money? Use cheque book and Eurocheque card at a bank to obtain cash. (Make out cheque in sterling – they will do the conversion.) Look for shops displaying Eurocredit symbol where you can use your credit card. If not in Europe, look for a job! British Consul is absolutely last resort and even then may not show interest.

15 Camp sites

Trailer caravanners and tent owners naturally regard camp sites and their location, their facilities and their fees, as all-important. To judge by their conversation, and the letters they write to magazines, many motor caravanners hold the same view. But there are many others who never go near one. Is the camp site, then, essential to the motor caravanner? Is it merely sometimes useful? Or is it completely dispensable?

From the legal viewpoint, camping and caravan sites are most certainly essential. The public highway is not intended as a dormitory. Parked by the side of a road – or for that matter in a carpark or a layby – the position of a motor caravan not being used as means of transport is at best ambiguous. Although a number of arguments can be deployed in the motor caravanner's favour, he would be unwise to be drawn into using them. This is a case where discretion is almost invariably the better part of valour. If told by anyone with a suggestion of authority to move on, he would be wiser to do just that. There will probably be a more suitable place to park a mile or two further on.

The motor caravan outside a camp site is there by grace and favour. In a sense it is the existence of sites which makes 'wild' camping possible. Without them motor caravans would only exist on the margins of the law. That point having been made, it remains true that grace and favour can go a long way. Even in Great Britain the discreet motor caravanner, choosing his night's resting place with common sense, asking permission where possible and convenient, and humbly complying with the directions of authority on the rare occasions it impinges on his activities, can travel the length and breadth of the island without going near a site.

Although the technical legalities are remarkably similar in many countries abroad, the chances of his being disturbed or even inconvenienced there are even less. In the first place there is generally far more space available; in the second place there are far fewer motor caravans, so that there is less awareness amongst the authorities of their legal position; and in the third place there is a general desire to encourage the tourist, however unusual his mode of transport.

Considering the importance, at least in theory, of the camp site for motor caravans, it is remarkable that they were given such a churlish welcome in the early days. Some site wardens carefully segregated them away from trailer caravans, placing them amongst the tents. The most important chain of sites, that owned by the Caravan Club, kept them out altogether, and for a long time even denied membership to motor caravanners. When it at last saw the light, and membership and sites were thrown open, this official approval by 'Big Brother' led to general acceptance.

This initial reaction is perhaps responsible for a certain prejudice against sites amongst some motor caravanners. For one or two people permanent 'wild' camping is in fact very easy. Water to last a week can be taken on the average coachbuilt model. It can easily be renewed when travelling, and a nearby source is often available even when stationary. One's own sanitary arrangements are usually more hygienic than those on many sites. Supermarkets, and open-air fruit and vegetable markets, are almost invariably cheaper than camp shops. If one of the purposes of motor caravanning is to get away from it all, there seems little point in merely getting away to a site where one's neighbours are closer, and less avoidable, than at home.

Of course, there are arguments to be made in favour of sites. Anyone who has been in a motor caravan with more than one companion, or with small children, knows that getting up and washing in the morning can prove to be a long and tedious routine. The extra facilities provided on sites mean that this takes only a fraction of the time. Children will quickly make friends, and for the adults there is at once a lack of tension and a pleasant informality about neighbourly relationships which are known to be temporary.

Many sites are in splendid settings. If you stay at the Touring Club de France site beside the Seine in the Bois de Boulogne, in unspoilt parkland barely two miles from the Arc de Triomphe, with all the leading newspapers of Europe on sale each day at the well-stocked shop, and with pretty multi-lingual hostesses at the Information Bureau answering every conceivable question put to them by the constant stream of arrivals from all over Europe and from further overseas, you will probably feel more at the heart of things and better looked after than in one of the luxury hotels on the Champs Elysées. Waking up to untroubled Mediterranean sunshine on one of the new Spanish sites, walking beneath the pines for a swim and a sunbathe on the private beach while the children are looked after and entertained, and then wondering whether to use its excellent but inexpensive restaurant, or to prepare a lighter lunch yourself, you will probably pity the package tourists in their high-rise concrete boxes. Or you might wish to stay at one of the forty or so Castels et Camping sites attached to a French château, eating peaches and tomatoes sold at wholesale prices from the kitchen garden, reading in the dovecot which has been converted into a library, and enjoying an armagnac with the lord of the manor.

The sensible conclusion, as usual, is probably a compromise. Although it is not essential for the motor caravanner to stay on a site, he would be missing a great deal if he dispensed with them altogether. Even in its humblest form a site can provide a good clean-up for clothes and for the van itself, as well as for its occupants. At its best it can provide a memorable experience.

Even if he wishes to, he may not be able to use sites all the year round. In northern Europe they are often open only from about 1 June to 15 September. A typical season in central or southern France runs from Easter to mid-October. Even all-season sites, like those in Spain between Barcelona and Sitges, or at Benidorm, will probably close for a month a year to give their staff a holiday.

Although charges vary widely, within each country they generally conform to definite tariffs laid down by the authorities. These depend on the amenities available. In France, for example, they range from less than 3 francs per person and per *emplacement* for a one-star category site, offering little beyond toilets and drinking water, to 8 or 9 francs per person and per *emplacement* for a luxury site offering hot showers, swimming pool, television room, and organized games. Spanish sites, because they are more recently built and have ample amenities, and because land values are high, are sometimes more expensive. Britain has no such authorized scale. Sites charge what they like, and facilities tend to be below those on the Continent.

Lists of sites both in the UK and in Europe are obtainable from the various motor caravan, caravan, and camping clubs in this country, and from similar organizations abroad. Often the London offices of the national tourist ministries are also able to supply lists of sites in their countries, with up-to-date scales of fees, and with other details. Many camping and caravan magazines also review sites, criticizing and commending according to readers' experiences. But some of the most delightful sites I know are on none of these lists. And the very aspects of a site which appeal to some people may be just what others would wish to avoid.

So in general the motor caravanner should never book ahead. If a site is full he can spend the night in some quiet spot nearby. If it proves unsuitable – too crowded, too far from the beach, plagued by mosquitoes – he can move on. This is the freedom which a motor caravan gives. If, however, you wish to take your holiday close to the sea and during the high season, you should reserve a place on a site or you will never get in.

If you intend to holiday in Britain, you would be well advised to drive down to your chosen site for a trial weekend before booking. If you are going abroad, and have no word of mouth recommendation to go on, you could do worse than to attend the Camping Outdoor Holiday Exhibition and Motor Caravan Show held each January at Olympia. Several well-run continental sites, notably on the Spanish Mediterranean, take their own stands there. Prospective users can talk to the owners, as well as look at photographs, plans and models. They can make their reservations for particular plots there and then. And it seems unlikely that businessmen prepared to go to all that amount of trouble will want to disappoint their clients when they actually arrive on the site seven or eight months later.

16 Wild camping

If you have decided not to stay on an official site, or if it is off-season and the official sites are closed, what do you look for in an 'unofficial' one?

The first requirement is security. To a large extent this is subjective – you are as safe as you feel. When on my own, I personally prefer to be within reach of help in an emergency. I can sleep comfortably near a farm where I have asked permission to park, or near the home of friends. Often I draw up on one of those vast market squares which seem to lie behind even the most insignificant French villages. There I can happily drop off in a place I have never seen before, amongst people whom, if I drive off early enough, I may never meet.

In over twelve years, during which time I was motor caravanning for at least nine months a year – let us say in 3,000 nights – I was only disturbed once, and in Switzerland of all places. It was disturbance, not attack. I was awoken by a banging on the van at one in the morning, to hear laughter and retreating steps as I confusedly asked who wanted what.

In fact a reasonably able-bodied person alone in a motor caravan is many times safer than someone living on their own in more conventional housing. It is harder to force an entry into a van than into the average house, and its occupant is more quickly aroused. The attacker is more likely to attract attention, and to be acting in an even more suspicious manner than the ordinary housebreaker. A cry of alarm from inside the van will force him to run away to avoid recognition by neighbours. And what householder, when attacked, can walk into the front room and move his home to safety at up to sixty miles an hour?

It is really only to feel safe, and not because I believe that I might be running a risk, that I personally prefer not to sleep alone far from any habitation. If for any reason I do so, I am careful to draw my curtains, so that any passer-by is unaware that I am all by myself.

When accompanied, on the other hand, I have no hesitation in

The pleasures of wild camping are well illustrated by this British van enjoying the solitude of a Norwegian valley.

parking wherever I wish. There is not only safety in numbers, but, more important, a feeling of safety. One can then draw up in lonely forests, on stretches of disused roadway, by quiet lakes or deserted beaches.

Naturally I always ask permission if anyone is available. On the rare occasions when it is refused I move on. Not only does such permission give my parking a semblance of legality: it is often the prelude to a rewarding relationship. From such requests have I got to know the farmer, from whom I have later bought my milk and eggs, the proprietor of the cafe, where I have later received my mail, the forest verderer, who has later initiated me into the mysteries of his craft.

The greatest dangers for the motor caravanner in wild camping are neither human nor legal. They are physical. He must at all costs avoid getting stuck. That tempting grass verge may be heavy with dew. Those apparently hard-caked flats by the lake may be only the thin crust of a thick layer of mud. That woodland glade, complete with fallen trunks to act as dining table and chairs for alfresco meals, may be soft with humus.

Few coachbuilt models, fully loaded, weigh much less than

two tons, and even small conversions are heavier than the average saloon car. Once a wheel starts to spin, the process of extrication can be long and exhausting. Carefully timed reversing, putting down brushwood in the tracks, or laying down lengths of rubber sheeting, may do the trick. All motor caravanners would be wise to carry those specially manufactured diamond-mesh metal grids to place under the wheels. But if these endeavours are unsuccessful, the van may become bogged down deeper and deeper in its own tracks, and eventually it will be necessary to secure the assistance of another vehicle with a tow rope.

The experience is unpleasant and frustrating anywhere. But if it is far from where any friendly car or tractor may be expected to pass, it is a major disaster. So at all costs get out and test, or make one of your passengers get out and test any remotely suspicious surface. Consider, too, whether the ground, hard enough now, might be transformed into slithering mire by a night's downpour.

All the camping and caravan clubs have codes of behaviour which their members agree to respect. Most sites, too, have similar lists of *dos* and *don'ts*, posted at their entrance and sometimes circulated to each arrival. Not all are strictly relevant to the wild camper. For example, though he would not want to overwhelm the nocturnal quiet with noise, there is no reason why he should switch off his radio on the stroke of ten, as most sites rightly insist. And in the absence of drains he will have to empty his dirty water on the open ground.

But he should not treat litter in the same way. Rubbish of any sort should be as scrupulously collected, and either buried, or saved for disposal in a litter bin or on a refuse dump. And though clothes must obviously be dried, the bushes on which they are spread out, or the trees between which the clothes-line is strung, need not be the most visible. In short, he should avoid anything which might offend or smack of squalor, striving to be as neat and as unnoticeable as possible.

The same precepts should be followed even more rigorously when parking in cities. For wild camping is perfectly possible in an urban environment. Not every capital has a conveniently and beautifully situated site like that beside the Seine in the Bois de Boulogne.

A conveniently placed side street or carpark within walking distance of the main monuments can save pounds in public transport and site fees. I look back on a highly educational fortnight parked just off the Kärntner Ring in Vienna. I have enjoyed shorter stays in the residential district behind the Retiro park in Madrid, on the carpark on the island where the causeway ends at Venice, and even in those few streets near the South Bank of the Thames which are still free of parking meters. After a morning on your feet in museums, or doing business in the City, it makes all the difference to be able to put your legs up after lunch in your own home.

Airports and railway stations, with all their laid-on facilities – toilets, water taps, news-stands, waiting rooms, departure lounges – often make good bases in or near cities. Indeed railway stations, for the same reason, make good sites anywhere. In Italian hill country I have sometimes found that they offer the only parking spot away from the narrow, twisting road.

It is even possible to park in cities in lands such as North Africa, where wild camping is not otherwise to be recommended. These countries often have few official sites. But there carparks, and often whole streets, are patrolled by guards. These for a modest tip will protect the motor caravanner from disturbance during sleep, and his belongings from theft during absence. Outside cities he should only stay beside police stations (and after receiving permission), or with groups of several other campers or caravanners, such as are found all winter on the coast north of Agadir.

France, three times larger than Britain and with a smaller population, is the best country of all for wild camping – or indeed for any form of motor caravanning. It is only in France that one finds that occasional *Camping gratuit*, where a village a little off the beaten track has thrown open a field or common, in the hope of attracting a few extra customers for its shops and restaurants. Toilets, drinking water tap, and litter bins are generally laid on. And beside the placid Indre, amongst the oaks and bracken of central Brittany, or surrounded by the steep Beaujolais hillsides, I have enjoyed at once the security and convenience normally associated with an organized site, together with the inexpensiveness and freedom which belongs only to camping wild.

17 The motor caravan as a way of life

It is not only gipsies who live permanently in caravans. Once the motor caravan had been developed, it was only a question of time before someone adopted it as a whole way of life. As early as 1961 a lady, already approaching seventy, sold her lovely period house near Windsor and bought a Paralanian. Over the years I have heard of people meeting her – on cross-channel ferries, beside the Mediterranean, or on the edge of the Sahara – although my own path has yet to cross with hers. It is surprising that this has not happened, for I have chanced to run into for a second time all three of the couples whom I know possess no other home than a motor caravan.

Such re-encounters have become so frequent since I first began motor caravanning that I have long since rejected their unlikelihood. The reason is probably that people who travel a lot tend to follow certain routes, and to frequent certain places. Thomas Cook's office opposite the Madeleine Church in Paris, or the quayside at Algeciras, are just two out of a hundred examples. The frequency of such meetings means not only that the motor carvanner is always amongst friends – that goes without saying. It means also that he is often amongst old friends.

The first of the three meetings occurred after a gentleman had written to me out of the blue in the very early days of motor caravanning. He had read a letter of mine to *The Motor Caravanner*, in which I described how I had obtained very satisfactory motor insurance from a Spanish company. As he was about to retire to Spain, and knowing that he would be facing the same insurance problems as myself, he wondered if we could meet on his way to buy a flat on the Cantabrian coast.

So one August evening in 1962 we kept our rendezvous at the lighthouse which marks the point where the Pyrenees at last fall into the Atlantic, just at the frontier with France. I had an English and a French friend with me in the van, and many more friends amongst the Civil Guards and fishermen who frequented the lonely little bar there. So we made it a memorable occasion, enlivened all the more by a bottle of whisky donated by my new acquaintance. But he and his wife sat silent and reserved as we drank, sang, and even danced, cut off it seemed by temperament as well as the language barrier.

They also seemed to have difficulty in adapting to the motor caravanning life. Although at that time I had owned my first Highwayman for only nine months, I had rapidly adjusted to the limits of the possible and the desirable. I was horrified when, to make a cup of tea, he plugged in a specially adapted electric kettle to his engine battery.

Nor did they propose to use their Highwayman – a rather younger one than my own – for more than limited periods. They were on their way to a new property development on the north Spanish coast, where they intended to buy an apartment. This was to serve as their headquarters, and the van was to be used for two or three extended trips each year. As politely as possible I pointed out the high rainfall on the Cantabrian coast, and all the experiences they would be missing by not making the van a more permanent base. But as I waved goodbye next morning to the pleasant but portly pair, I was convinced that they would soon be returning to the suburbs from which they had come.

Five years later, in July 1967, I was at Dinard in the north of Brittany. Returning from the beach to my van I noticed a 1962 Highwayman parked alongside. Professional interest, as well as inborn curiosity, led me to peep into every window, walking round and round the vehicle as a horse-trainer will pace round the paddock before a race meeting. I was only brought to a halt by a good-natured shout from a café opposite: 'You can have it for £2,000.'

Making my way across the road I found a fit-looking middle-aged couple with their son and daughter-in-law seated round a table. They accepted my excuse for the curiosity I had been showing, and admitted that a few minutes earlier they had been taking an equal interest in my own van. The older man told me that he and his wife had been living in their van for the previous four years, mainly on the Mediterranean coast of Spain, but with one long trip up to the North Cape of Norway. Then, as I turned to go, we exchanged names.

Only then did I recognize in the bronzed, lithe pair, who did not look a day over fifty, the pale, tired couple I had met five years earlier, on the brink of retirement. I recalled our earlier meeting, the party, and our discussions.

They told me that when they had actually started going into the complications of house ownership in a foreign country, and at the same time found the motor caravanning way of life more and more satisfactory with every month that passed, they had decided to remain one hundred per cent mobile all the year round. And during the party in their van that evening, I noticed that numerous gadgets and fittings, of a more practical variety than kettles working off batteries, had been installed since that first party five years earlier.

Despite the frequency of such meetings it came as a shock when the man standing beside me outside a dentist's flat in Santa Cruz de Tenerife in the Canary Islands in March 1971 turned to me with a word of greeting. For although I had thought about him and discussed him a good deal in the previous seven years, he was the last person I had expected to see then and there.

We had met early in 1964 in Tenerife, when we were drawn together by our motor caravans. Both were Bluebird Highwaymen, and both were on the Morris J2 chassis, that grand old warhorse which made up in dependability for any deficiencies in performance or noise levels. His was of 1962 vintage – the period when Highwaymen were fitted with two windows on each side, and a Perspex roof which could be raised at all four corners. Mine was almost out of the Ark – a 1960 model – and we had both acquired them when they were about eighteen months old, for exactly the same figure of £610.

Fond though I was of mine, I have to admit that he probably had the better bargain. My roof was fixed, so that I knew what it was to be hot in summer. The previous owner of his had effected numerous improvements, especially in the way of extra shelves and curtains, so that both the cab and the rear end of the caravan could be screened off. We had an interesting time during that winter, comparing notes on the frequent occasions when our paths crossed as we explored the island.

He was even newer to the open-air life than I was, and had set himself higher, or as I would have preferred to put it, more complicated standards. In my heart of hearts I did not for one moment believe that he and his charming, very feminine wife, would last on the open road for more than a few months. And when they spent several nights in a hotel in Santa Cruz, and later took a furnished house on a longish lease, I subconsciously crossed them off my list of people I expect to see again. It appeared obvious that they needed roots.

When, after a full minute, I had taken in who it was standing next to me, I asked, though I felt sure I knew the answer, what had happened to the Highwayman. He told me that it was parked on the quayside, and after we had made our appointments he took me along to a Highwayman which looked not a day older than it had done seven years earlier. They explained how they had had it resprayed two years before, and that their total milage was no more than 5,000 a year. This had extended the life not only of the van itself, but of its accessories. Since I had met them they had needed only one change of tyres, and one new battery.

It certainly looked as though the slow pace they had adopted was lengthening their own lives as well. Both looked five years younger than when last I had seen them. I told them so. He explained that before he first bought his motor caravan he had been working very hard in the north, pushing himself and no doubt subjecting himself to continuous stress for year after year. When I had seen him he was in process of unwinding, which itself was a shock. For this reason he had taken that furnished house. But the sunshine and the peace had soon put him right. They had sub-let the house and moved back into the van before midsummer. And they had never left it since.

And then they began to tell me where they had been. Their story illustrated something I have proved for myself: that the years when one clocks up least miles are years when one does most travelling. The big distances, the heavy petrol bills, the wear on the engine and on one's own body, come from those dashes to the Mediterranean for a fortnight's holiday. Even those four-month winter trips to sunnier climes enjoyed by so many retired couples can involve covering an awful lot of ground.

But this couple, having spent a leisurely three months in Tuscany, moved gently on for an equally leisurely three months in Provence. And when they went to Morocco, instead of fitting everything into a few frantic weeks, they enjoyed the winter at Agadir, the spring at Marrakech, and then moved up to the temperate Middle Atlas for the summer!

It was not long before we were once again comparing notes. It was nice to find that our discussions were more harmonious than at our earlier meetings. Obviously our points of view were now closer. I, though unaware of the fact until then, was prepared to make greater allowance for 'gracious living'. They, for their part, had seen the wisdom of dropping many non-essentials and the problems that accompany them. They enthusiastically approved of the way I had swopped my refrigerator with a Spanish carpenter in return for work he had done on my interior, and of my purchase of plastic bowls for washing and for washing up after my Perspex sink had smashed.

They too had been busy getting rid of things rather than acquiring them. Some of these were eminently sensible. For example, as I first stepped inside he asked me to clean the soles of my shoes with the brush hanging just inside the door. He explained how they had lost their doormat, and soon found that they were better off without it. The dust and dirt were always falling through it, and then being carried further into the van. Now they made sure it never got inside in the first place. My own doormat was due for renewal; and following their example I replaced it by a hook between door and wardrobe for my brush.

Some of their simplifications, on the other hand, struck me as tempting fate. They had deliberately thrown away their starting handle, their jack, and even their spare wheel! He said that he had been driving since 1928, and had never needed any of them. My only comment is that some people are born lucky.

The reason why he had disposed of these tools was to save weight. He found the J2's 1489 cc engine underpowered, and becoming a little more so with every year. When they drove up to Las Cañadas, a lunar wasteland 7,000 ft above sea level in the centre of Tenerife, he deliberately unloaded all their luggage, and many accessories, including even the spare bunk with its heavy supporting poles. These, along with his wife, travelled separately by taxi!

Weight was also one reason why he preferred, like myself, one-gallon plastic jerricans for his water supply, instead of a large tank with pump. He found them easier to fill and to clean, and preferred not to be dependent on taps or hoses, but able to take on water at any wayside spring or pump. Like me, too, he had often used his jerricans for other drinks: health-giving waters from lonely spas, and wine at a few pence a litre straight from the vineyard.

The present Highwayman, of course, is based on the Commer 1725 cc engine. But I, too, once owned the earlier model on the Morris J2, and had never found it underpowered. I asked him if he expected a great deal more performance than myself.

He at once denied this, telling me that he never travelled more than 30 miles an hour. And it was several years since they had travelled more than a hundred miles in a day. There was no need for hurry, when they had all the time in the world. Where they were a bit hard on the old J2 was in loading it up with luggage. For with no home behind them, they had to carry an awful lot around. Some of it they left in store whenever possible. At that moment they had three big suitcases in Santa Cruz, which they had left when they landed, a trunk with a friend in Barcelona, and half a dozen tea chests in a depository in Zurich. Finding a permanent home for all this stuff was a secondary reason why they were looking around to buy a house, though they could not make up their minds where it was going to be. They knew the whole of Europe, and knew that at certain seasons even the Côte d'Azur and the Algarve had their snags. Having lived a few years in a motor caravan, moving on whenever the weather or the spirit moved them, the prospect of settling anywhere for good was not very attractive. Of course, they would still have the van for long holidays. But the nuisance of having a house to look after and to go back to would always be at the back of their minds. However, they had got to buy one all the same, he assured me grimly.

I asked why. There was no law forcing him to be a property owner. They could soon get rid of their goods in store if they really wanted to. In any case, these were only the secondary reasons. Whatever was the main reason for his having to buy a house again?

If his answer had not left me speechless, I would have burst out laughing. With a face like a mourner he told me that seven years of travelling in a motor caravan had enabled them to save so much money that they had to find somewhere to invest it.

It was November 1971 when I met my third couple at Seo de

Urgel, the little Spanish Pyrenean town whose bishop is Co-Prince of neighbouring Andorra. The first snow of the winter had just fallen, and the French police had turned me back from the usual approach to Andorra, across the 8,000 ft Envalira Pass. So I had gone 'the long way round' through Bourg-Madame, and decided to stop at Seo before driving up to Andorra the following day. Pulling into the empty carpark which I had often used before, on the edge of the town, I was pleased to see a GB Roadranger.

The curtains were drawn, and I made no attempt to disturb the occupants. But I was delighted when, just as it was getting dark, a middle-aged man in cap and Burberry knocked on the door, and enquired whether I would like to join them for a coffee later on, after dinner.

It proved a long and interesting evening, and as coffees and brandies were drunk, my host and his wife told me about themselves. On his retirement from the Services, he had taken a job in the City, and endeavoured to reconcile himself to a life geared to the 8.17. His wife's friends imagined that she would be glad to settle down at last to a permanent home.

But throughout her exciting postings in Malta and Aden and Hong Kong, she had never had the time to long for a permanent home. And it was not only the absence of servants which made the chore-filled reality less of a delight than her friends expected. It was the climate. It was the narrowing of everyday social contacts, and above all the boredom of spending fifty weeks a year in the same place.

Inevitably, they took their annual holidays abroad. But even then, they were irked by the frustrations of package-tour hotel life, when compared with the satisfactions of shopping as they had once done in the exotic markets.

Their moment of revelation came in 1962 in Northern Spain, when on their morning walk they had gone as far as they safely could if they were to be back at their hotel at the hour fixed for lunch. They happened to be just level with the entry to a camp site, and the husband gave a sudden sniff. The smell intrigued him. He had never thought that anything really appetizing could be cooked outside a proper kitchen. He suggested that before they turned back, they should have a walk round the tents and caravans, to see how these campers coped.

As they saw the happy families and contented couples, in jeans and bikinis, stirring their stews or washing their salads, the open-air informality, and the crisp convenience of the caravans, they turned to each other in astonishment. What were they doing with all those starchy bores in the hotel? This was where they belonged.

The next summer they crossed the Channel towing a Sprite Alpine. The venture was a total success. During the year which followed, their dreams and their waking thoughts were alike devoted to planning their next trip. As they again returned home, and to a life which spelled neither contentment nor commitment, they at last discussed what had long been at the back of their minds.

What were they doing it all for? Their son was no longer at home. Their house meant no more to the wife than the job in the City did to the husband. After all the tax, he was almost paying to work. Living on his pension in the caravan they would be better off.

So he retired for a second time. They let the house, and set off. Since then they had only made two alterations to their way of life; and both only went to prove its success.

The first was to change their car and trailer for a motor caravan. They quoted all the reasons to be found elsewhere in this book. In particular they stressed the compactness, the greater load-carrying capacity, the possibility of placing bookshelves and other installations on the more rigid walls, and the reduced ferry charges.

The second alteration, and one they had only just made that first time we met, was to sell their house. In order not to create a protected tenancy, they had only let it on short-term, furnished leases. Their problems had been legion. As they returned each spring to an uncut lawn, damaged furniture, unpaid rents and rocketing rates, they thought with regret of the sunnier climes which they might be enjoying without this incubus. So they gave their son the pick of the furniture, sent the rest to the auction room, stored with friends a couple of trunks full of belongings which they wished to retain, and put the house on the market.

They had no regrets about their decision. But they were naturally conscious that they had burned their boats, and were glad to be away from more conventional 'friends' who never stopped reminding them of the fact. Our evening together strengthened us both in our allegiance to the motor caravan as a way of life. I waved goodbye next morning as they set off for Portugal, certain that we would meet again somewhere, sometime.

We did so earlier than I had expected. At the end of January 1974 I left Marrakesh after six happy weeks camping amidst some friends' orange groves, spent a few days parked beneath the ramparts of the ancient port of Mogador, and then set off one morning down the coast.

About thirty miles before Agadir lies a cape, after which the shoreline bends at right angles, and runs to the south of the Atlas Mountains. Along this protected strip, which I was approaching for the first time, I knew that many hundreds of motor caravanners came to spend the worst months of winter.

A few miles after the cape I saw the first group of them: five vans within easy calling distance of one another for security. They were on a ledge twenty feet below the road, but above high-water mark. Pulling into the side, I climbed down to collect my first impressions of motor caravanning on the shores of Southern Morocco.

The New Zealand couple with whom I first got into conversation persuaded me to join the group for at least a night. After I had parked my van I accepted an invitation to their VW, outside which stood a table spread with cups and saucers, biscuits and cheese sandwiches. I was not their only guest. The other woman who was sitting there told me that her husband had a very good eye for a van, and that he had recognized my Highwayman from our meeting at Seo de Urgel. He was busy fishing at that moment, but he would have plenty of opportunities of talking to me in the days to come. And she there and then invited me into their Roadranger for coffee that evening.

After such a welcome my stay with that friendly little group was naturally extended, and I returned several times to spend the odd night or two with them after sorties to Agadir, and to all the exciting places further south, in the Anti-Atlas and the deep Sahara.

That couple had become the two most perfectly adapted motor caravanners I have had the pleasure to know. They took delight in every aspect of the life: barbecue lunches of grilled sardines shared in the blazing February sun with other members of the group; bartering for eggs or loaves with the robed Moroccans who wandered up and down the coast supplying the motor caravanners; the after-dinner coffees and brandies in their van or someone else's; the weekly trips to Agadir to pick up mail, shop, and call on friends at the crowded camp site at Taghazoute-Plage on their return route; her swimming; his fishing. They taught me several useful tricks: how to improve my radio reception by an aerial made out of any old length of wire; how to combine gracious living, closer cosiness, and battery saving by the use of candles; and even how to make a professional job out of painting a van.

Because Southern Morocco is the most accessible region with a warm winter, they tended to find their way there for the four coldest months. Camping in North Africa requires greater prudence than in Europe. And the security which comes from having everything, oneself included, in a single vehicle, more than ever confirmed them in their decision to opt for a motor caravan.

As our three couples above have shown, finance tends to be less of a worry to those living permanently in motor caravans than to those in houses. Assuming that they have an income from somewhere – and without it they are hardly likely to adopt the life in the first place – they will probably after a few years have more finances to worry about than those who have stayed at home. For income which is not spent has a happy habit of accumulating.

Anyone who is, or who becomes, a non-resident of the United Kingdom can purchase his motor caravan free of VAT and Car Tax. It will bear a number plate surrounded by a yellow line. (The appropriate Customs and Excise Notice to read is No. 705.) When returning to Britain the non-resident will be issued by Customs at the port of entry with a form No. 115D. This entitles him to keep the vehicle in Britain for up to twelve months, without having to pay Road Tax, and without being obliged to put his van, if more than three years old, through the MOT test. Form 115D also specifies that the van must not be sold, hired, or driven by anyone other than the owner before it is re-exported.

A motor caravanner who emigrates permanently to another land, on the other hand, will sooner or later have to import and

register his van into his new country of residence, with considerable formalities and expense, and with high rates of duty.
It is true that other countries, too, have systems of tax-free
sales to non-residents. German cars bearing oval-shaped number
plates, and French cars whose registrations include the letters
'TT', have been purchased in this way. But the German cars must
be permanently exported within twelve months, and the French
vehicles within six. Only a British car can circulate indefinitely
abroad, and periodically revisit its country of origin without
paying tax or duty.

Mail

The post, normally a source of mild interest or of less mild
irritation, is for the motor caravanner an indispensable lifeline.
Sometimes it can be quite literally vital: when a money order is
on its way to pay for the food and petrol, or when a telegram is
expected announcing the result of an operation. But even in less
critical moments it serves to keep him in touch not only with a
particular local scene, but with a whole world.

Mail must be considered from two separate points: the sending
end and the receiving end. Starting with the first, who is to do
the forwarding?

The ideal person is a trusted neighbour, friend or relative,
prepared to pick up the mail at regular and frequent intervals,
and to forward it to the latest address. For although the British
Post Office is prepared to forward mail for a fee, this is only to a
single address. When the van moves on, a fresh fee must be paid.
Arranging for payment is obviously a nuisance if you are abroad.

Personal forwarding has two further advantages. The Post
Office can only send on everything, regardless of contents. The
friend or neighbour, following instructions, can exercise greater
discretion, forwarding, say, private letters and financial
documents, where some action is required, and stockpiling mere
advertising brochures and company reports.

He or she can also ensure that every letter forwarded bears the
correct postage. I have known motor caravanners who have
always had all their mail automatically forwarded abroad without ever suffering a postal surtax. But they have been exceptionally lucky. Everything depends on the local postal authorities
abroad. If they are aware of the cost of sending letters from

Britain to Europe they will clap a surtax, often at double the value of the missing stamps, on a letter franked with any less. Several pence extra for every letter received can be an annoying drain, especially during those periods when there are severe restrictions on the amount of foreign exchange permitted for travellers outside Britain.

The intelligent friend or neighbour would at the same time make sure that stamps were not added unnecessarily. Thus, letters from foreign countries have already paid their own appropriate postage for abroad, and can be forwarded as they stand. For most weights, too, the rate for printed papers overseas is actually less than within the UK, enabling club journals or magazines bought on subscription to be sent on by surface mail at no further cost.

To many readers these details may already be getting a little obscure. Some may be wondering if they can find anyone sufficiently intelligent, and with whom they are sufficiently intimate, to carry out such a complex and confidential routine. Apart from a neighbour or the Post Office they have two alternatives to whom they might delegate the task of forwarding.

The first is the local branch of their own bank. They and their affairs are familiar to the staff. Few branches are without one or more customers abroad – people who have emigrated to Australia, or been posted to an Italian subsidiary – and therefore know how to deal with mail for overseas. Above all they have the Securities Departments, whose trained staffs know how to sift through the Company Reports and the Allotment Letters, the Share Certificates and the Rights Issues, the Pension cheques, the Life Assurance Premium requests, and perhaps even the Surtax Demands. According to their instructions they can deal with many of these themselves and can either stockpile or destroy whatever requires no action. They need then only forward those documents which actually require personal attention. Most banks will make a charge for this service, which will vary from branch to branch. .

The second alternative is to channel all mail through a specialist in forwarding. These are almost invariably in London, which should make for less delay – provided that there is no shortage of sorters in such postal districts as W1. Amongst these specialists are certain banks. The 'Overseas' branches of some of the

British clearing banks in the West End or the City certainly have the experience, and might be prepared to arrange forwarding once an account had been opened with them.

Certain of the London branches of the Commonwealth banks have complete Mail Departments, specially set up to forward the mail of their customers visiting Europe. Because so many of these customers are youngsters, whose accounts are barely profitable, they often charge a fee of two or three pounds a year. But as a result of this fee, their forwarding service is generally open to non-customers too.

The advantage of this service is that it is professional. A personal Mail Service Number is allotted, to be added to mail sent to the bank, so that there is no risk of letters going to another client with the same name. Printed Change of Address forms are provided, to be sent in as appropriate. Unlike the Post Office redirection service, therefore, forwarding addresses can be altered whenever convenient. The Bank can also 'hold' mail until a new address has been found.

On the other hand there can be no really detailed instructions, and no checking of postage. But in practice I have yet to pay any postal surtax on mail forwarded by the particular bank I use – perhaps the bank's prestige has something to do with this!

The greatest specialist of all in forwarding is even more professional, and even more personal. British Monomarks also operate from Central London, where subscribers are offered not only a mail forwarding service, but a mail desk to call at, private post boxes, telephone answering, a private cable address, and use of a Telex.

Their distinctive feature is the allocation of an individual Monomark to each subscriber. By special arrangement with the Post Office this is sufficient to find him, even without the addition of his name, from anywhere in the world. (Hence a British Monomark is often given as the address for reply to anonymous advertisements.)

The first part of each Monomark reads 'BM/', but what follows can be as the subscriber chooses, provided that it does not duplicate another already registered. Thus possible choices by the writer might be: 'BM/MYHILL', 'BM/MOTOR CARAVAN', 'BM/HIGHWAYMAN', 'BM/YXL 671' (once my van's number), followed always by 'London W1CV 6XX'.

Mail and messages can be held at The British Monomark offices at 24–27 High Holborn, or can be sent to meet subscribers as they travel. Instructions may be changed as often as wished, by letter, telephone or cable. There is a special Cable Code enabling speedy and complete instructions to be conveyed in a single word. Thus, 'FOUR' requests the forwarding of letters and printed matter, but not of parcels, in a single batch, after which subsequent mail is to be held until further instructions are sent.

Inevitably all this service has to be paid for. Charges include so many pounds a year for the registration of a personal Mono-mark, so much for each letter collected from the offices, so much for each letter redirected, and of course extra postage if forward-ing is to be by airmail or 're-enclosed'.

These problems at the sending end are less than half the story. For we come now to where the motor caravanner should receive his mail. Before going into any details I make one sug-gestion: that he changes his address as infrequently as possible, and with the maximum advance notice. Otherwise his letters will have to be forwarded on from one address to the next. And if a trusted, intelligent friend or relative can make mistakes in forwarding, it can be imagined how these can be compounded by some bare acquaintance speaking a foreign language.

The Poste Restante would at first sight seem the simplest and most satisfactory place to pick up letters. Almost every village has a post office, and the people who keep them understand the importance of mail. Unfortunately, most post offices now levy a charge for this service. During a recent visit to the Dordogne, when my friends from whom I would normally have collected mail were overseas, I found myself paying well over £1 a week at the post office simply to pick up my *courrier*.

The traditional mail boxes for travellers abroad have been the offices of Thomas Cook and of their associate Wagons-Lits/ Cook, and of American Express. Cook's, I know, continue the service mainly for the publicity it gives their name. For a century now characters in novels have been collecting their mail from Cook's.

Unfortunately the offices of these two companies are a little thin on the ground outside the main tourist areas. And both now make a charge of one or two dollars for re-forwarding. American Express also insist that everyone using their mail service uses also some of their other services (such as, for example, carrying their travellers' cheques).

Certain camps – in France the Touring Club de France sites, or the big residential sites like Le Pin de la Lègue near Fréjus – are very good at handling mail. But other sites can be indescribably cavalier in their treatment of correspondence. And many motor caravanners never use organized sites.

Friends can of course be invaluable. So can a friendly café, a shop where the motor caravanner habitually makes purchases, or even a remote farm near which he is wild camping.

Best of all is perhaps a small local bank. Permission can be asked personally on arrival, until which time mail is 'held' at home. But sometimes the traveller is planning a ten days' journey, and is anxious that mail should await him on arrival. A suitable bank at the town of destination can then be found in the bank directory, a copy of which will be found in all moderately sized branches. A letter can be sent to the manager, telling him that the traveller will be using his branch when in the vicinity, and would be very grateful if he could receive his mail there during his stay.

On arrival there may well be a murmur of interest as he reveals his identity at the local branch of the Banco de Bilbao, the Crédit Lyonnais or the Banco di Santo Spirito. For it is surprising how many bank employees are keen collectors of foreign stamps. And when he decides to move on a couple of hundred miles, they will be only too glad to give him a note of introduction to the next local branch of the Banco de Bilbao, the Crédit Lyonnais, or the Banco di Santo Spirito, and to forward there whatever mail may arrive after his departure.

Reading and other objectives in travel

To that question so often posed by those leading normal, busy lives: 'When shall I ever find time to do any reading?', the best answer is 'Buy a motor caravan'.

For if we had not already given our vehicle so many other definitions, we could describe it as a miraculous manufacturer of leisure. And if any one activity is peculiarly well-suited to the motor caravanning way of life, that activity is reading.

Indeed, so much time is available that reading matter can be consumed at an unexpectedly rapid pace. Books, magazines and newspapers take up that most precious commodity – space. This can be conserved in two ways: by careful selection of the reading matter carried, and by its renewal *en route*.

Careful selection means the choice of paperbacks rather than heavier, more expensive hard-backed volumes. But paperbacks are not necessarily light fiction. A diet of nothing but ephemeral novels soon proves indigestible, and the inclusion of more serious books can make all the difference to a rainy week on the Costa Blanca, or to the two months waiting for the ship from Calcutta to Australia.

Now, too, is the time for developing a particular interest or hobby. Take away the background literature on Chinese porcelain, Balinese dancing, local government law, or the American West. You will return less of an amateur and more of an expert. Reading lists on any subject are available from the National Book League, Albemarle Street, London W1, if you join as a member.

If you are going to be something more than a passing tourist, why not get to know the countries where you will be staying? Those contemplating several months in Spain, for example, might start with William C. Atkinson's Pelican *Short History of Spain and Portugal*, or with those essential and enchanting books by Gerald Brenan: *South from Granada*, *The Face of Spain*, and *The Spanish Labyrinth*. It makes such a change from listening to half-formulated theories and second-hand experiences. Moreover you will soon find that it is towards *you* that the whole party turns when some problem of local custom or politics is raised.

The simplest method of renewing reading matter *en route* is to swop books. I recall a couple at Marrakesh one sunny winter, who from ten in the morning to six at night used to lie outside their vans reading. About twenty yards away – far enough for them not to be disturbed, yet near enough for them to keep an eye on it – lay a large panier half-filled with volumes. Against it leaned a square of cardboard bearing the inscription: PAPERBACKS TO SWOP. All too many of its contents were of the naked lady variety – I found this couple, like many others, thankful to borrow non-fiction works. But in places where numerous motor and trailer caravanners gather, such a simple system is not without its attractions. In many such places there is also a notice board, where books for swopping can be advertised as easily as unwanted awnings or gas appliances.

Some of the English libraries abroad also exchange paperbacks. Whether or not they charge a fee depends largely on whether they are one of the older libraries attached to the British churches in the longer-established resorts like Menton or Alassio, or whether they are one of the small commercial libraries serving the newer English-speaking colonies, especially on the Spanish Mediterranean.

The older, church-attached libraries can be a tremendous help to the motor caravanner. Although part of their stock often dates from as far back as the last century they do regularly acquire more recent books, which may also be donated by members of the local retired colony after they have finished with them. Sometimes, as at Dinard, they are open all day long and unattended. More often, as at Biarritz, they are open one afternoon a week, when the local British community gathers to change their books over a cup of tea.

A final method of renewal is to have parcels of books posted from home. Pick up your paperbacks before you leave at 5p or less a time at local second-hand bookshops or even rummage sales. Pack them up in *unsealed* parcels weighing just under the maximum allowed for the special reduced rate for printed papers. They can be posted off by a kind neighbour, when you are getting towards the end of your original reading matter, to wherever your van has reached (or to wherever your van will have reached, for a few weeks must be allowed for arrival). You can then either present your original stock of paperbacks to the local English Church library, give them to friends you have made abroad, or swop them.

I do not advise motor caravanners to join such private circulating libraries as the London Library. I have found that the nuisance and expense of posting books back for exchange, or when they are called in for use by some other subscriber, outweigh the superficial attractions of their facilities.

One book which should be in every motor caravan – but never swopped or given away – is a good one-volume encyclopedia. The *Petit Larousse*, for example, which now has an English edition, can serve at once as dictionary, atlas, and reference work on everything from Romanesque Art to World War II.

If you cannot do without your daily newspaper when you are abroad, you will probably find that the foreign papers, however educative their study, are no substitute. An English paper, and especially a Sunday one, can prove to be expensive, that is, if you can actually find one outside one of the bigger towns or resorts. So it is worth remembering that the *Daily Telegraph* has an exceptionally cheap overseas subscription service, both by air and by surface mail. It even provides a special bulk air-freight service to Paris, and papers are then sent on by ordinary mail all over the country.

Indeed the cheapest self-indulgence I know is to walk from the remote Pyrenean river or Breton lake, beside which I am camped, to the nearest farmhouse, to collect not only my litre of fresh milk, but also the previous day's *Daily Telegraph*. It will have cost me only a fraction more than if I had bought it in the bustle and pollution of Fleet Street itself.

Before moving on from reading matter, I must mention the most widely read motor caravanning book yet published, John Steinbeck's *Travels with Charley*, although this can be read as one long confession of failure. Anxious to get close to the heart of America, he had an early motor caravan specially built. It was a vehicle with every comfort, but it was so heavy that it did great damage to his original tyres. Yet he had qualms about leaving his familiar background of home and wife. All too frequently (to my mind) he put up for the night at motels, not so much for the convenience, as for the company they offered. One sometimes wonders whether he could have succeeded in completing his tour right round the States had he not had the friendship of his dog, the Charley of the title, to sustain him. And it is significant that this revealing travelogue had no sequel.

Apart from reading, there are, of course, many other leisure activities that can be enjoyed in a motor caravan. Photography, and various forms of collecting, for example, fit in well with the life, and there are many other more specialist activities and hobbies, which are not mentioned here because they can only appeal to a minority of readers. Some pursuits, such as painting, require a good deal of storage space. But anyone sufficiently keen on his own hobby will somehow find room for his equipment.

However, there is one interest for which the motor caravan

might have been specifically invented: the learning of foreign languages. Here I speak from experience. In the only modern language I was taught at school – French – I was always bottom of the class. Now, thanks to my motor caravan, I speak six languages.

A motor caravan can take you deep into the heart of a country, far from the sound of English. You will pick up the language not only by listening and talking to the residents, but by tuning in to the local radio stations. The news is one of the easiest programmes to follow, and it can be interesting to see how the French, the Germans or the Spaniards view a particular situation or event.

In every European country many of the universities run courses specially designed to teach foreigners their language and culture. Sometimes these are for a month or two in the summer, when the university would otherwise be closed. Sometimes they are held during the ordinary terms, when the foreigner can mingle with the ordinary students, and join in their activities. Such courses usually offer not only the language classes, but also lectures on the country's art and history, as well as opportunities to strike up friendships with fellow foreign students from all over the world.

A Student's Card is issued, which generally entitles its holder to free entry to all state museums, collections, and archaeological sites, reduced fares on the state railway system, and use of the subsidised university restaurants. These vary in quality from the rather monotonous *Mensa* fare at German universities, to the three course meals with wine, and choice of four tasty main dishes provided at Portuguese universities. The card can also be used at other university restaurants, not only in the country concerned, but throughout Europe and the world.

No academic qualifications are normally required for entry to these courses. Fees vary widely, although they are invariably lower than those at British universities and language schools. This is due to the laws of supply and demand: more people want to learn English. Because of this, a country whose language is less popular will tend to charge less, yet offer more. Thus, a year's tuition at Lisbon university costs only about a third of the price of a single month's summer course at a French university.

Italy is so keen that her language should recapture some of the international prestige it held during the Renaissance that it has a special University for Foreigners, the Università degli Stranieri, at Perugia in the heart of beautiful Umbria. The motor caravanner can sign on for a month at a time whenever he arrives. Placed in the beginners' class, he will be taught in Italian, and indeed will be surprised to find himself talking Italian, on his very first day. If he wishes he can attend lectures on the poetry of Dante, the art of Michelangelo, or the history of Venice.

At weekends he can camp a few miles away at Gubbio or Assisi. Eating his spaghetti at the University restaurant, he may find himself talking to an engineering student from Calabria, an American graduate researcher, an Iranian learning Italian so that he can study electronics at Rome, or a Swedish girl preparing a thesis on Mannerist art. And he will not be surprised that his class contains a number of Australians in self-converted VWs. For Lloyd Triestino has given them a discount of 70% on their return fares to Europe, provided that they spend a minimum of three months studying at Perugia.

These courses need not necessarily be for adults only. At universities in Italy, Austria, France and Spain I have met whole families learning a language together having arrived there in their motor caravans.

18 The motor caravanner's world

1 Great Britain

For the British resident the advantages of touring in his own country are obvious: no water to cross; no foreign currency to buy; no language difficulties; no need to stock up with food-stuffs because they are dearer abroad. Comparing relative costs he will also have a cheaper holiday. Only a few enclaves like the Channel Islands, Andorra and Ceuta have cheaper petrol than Britain. It is more expensive even in Italy and Morocco, where coupons are issued to tourists. Ferry charges are a heavy over-head on any journey overseas. And the total distance covered in Britain will probably be less than on the Continent.

The first disadvantage, the climatic one, is so obvious as to require no elaboration. But remember that the whole Atlantic seaboard of Europe, from the North Cape to Gibraltar, is also blessed with rain, and that Scandinavia enjoys 'fresher' summer nights.

The second disadvantage is that staying in one's own country is less of a change, or a *dépaysement*, as the French so lucidly put it. One way round this is to explore a chosen region in greater depth, with the aid of such tools as the Shell Guides, and the great Penguin county by county survey of British architecture by Nikolaus Pevsner.

The third, perhaps unexpected disadvantage is that Britain is the first country in Europe where the motor caravan has become really popular. The converse of the fact that they have more friends here than elsewhere is that they have, propor-tionately at least, more enemies too. There are more vans about, and authorities and officials have done more to regulate when and where they can park. For this reason the British motor caravanner feels more inhibited, less free, on his own roads than beyond the Channel.

But he will have more personal friends in Britain than abroad; and many of those friends, unlike the flat-dwelling Continentals, will have gardens with driveways. So remember that the motor

The peace still to be found in crowded Britain is here being enjoyed by motor caravanners beside a Scottish loch.

caravanner is an almost invariably welcome guest, who does not need a bed made up for him, and who can cook his own breakfast or other meals. A highly successful holiday can thus be spent using friends' homes as bases, with all the interest of entering briefly into their lives, but without the guilty knowledge that one is disturbing them.

The final disadvantage is Britain's density of population, greater than that of any other European country except Holland, Belgium and West Germany. Over much of the country it is hard to escape from the sights and sounds of urban living. Unlike the three overcrowded countries mentioned above, however, Britain enjoys peripheral wildernesses in the 'Celtic fringe' of the north and west. But these have already been well and truly discovered. All the cars and caravans of England seem to be trundling along the narrow roads of the Scottish Highlands in summer. And the rape of Cornwall is well-known and widely commented upon.

However, certain intermediate regions, so short of facilities as to be inaccessible to mass tourism, have been unjustly but fortunately neglected. Few but the motor caravanner – and none like the motor caravanner – can enjoy the deep peace still to be found in the Border Country of the bare Cheviots, in the Southern Uplands and by the Solway Firth, in the Welsh Marches, or in the Norfolk Breckland.

2 Ferries

Living on an island has its advantages, as was proved in 1588, in 1804, and in 1940. But the water which protects has also to be crossed by those who wish to visit the wider world. The motor caravanner who does this even once a year will find the car ferry is certainly his biggest single standing charge after his motor insurance.

The giant ferry operator is Sealink, the combined shipping fleet of British Rail, French Railways, ALA Steamship Company, Belgian Maritime Transport Authority, and the Dutch Zealand Steamship Company. Although in a sense under public ownership, it is run on commercial lines. And it has a number of private competitors, including European Ferries and Hoverlloyd.

Yet there is no difference in fares between these competitors when they ply the same routes. Inevitably, therefore, there is much talk of 'price fixing', and of the Channel being the most expensive crossing in the world. In defence the ferry operators can claim that no sheet of water so wide is crossed so frequently or at so many points. Their profitability has enabled them to introduce the drive-on, drive-off ferries to replace the crane-loading steamers, which caused many a motor caravanner in the past to miss a heart-beat as he watched his vehicle swinging high above the dock.

The motor caravanner has one great advantage over the ordinary motorist. Because he carries his house on his back he can afford to be very elastic about time. If he does miss a particular sailing, or cannot get on one, it is not the end of the world. There is no hotel room booked somewhere in the middle of France or Belgium, perhaps only the first in a chain of resting places. He can settle down to a cup of tea, write a few letters, or even have a night's sleep.

Provided that time is a truly secondary consideration, there is no real need for him to book his reservation in advance. All through July and August Sealink alone are running nine or ten departures a day from Dover to Calais. If there is no room on the first sailing, therefore, it will be only a couple of hours until the next, when he will be at the head of the queue.

For some of the less frequent, privately-run services, such as the Bergen Line from Newcastle to Bergen, Brittany Ferries from Plymouth to Roscoff, or Swedish Lloyd from Southampton to Bilbao, prior reservation is more important. Since the steep rise in petrol prices some of these more offbeat services have become of great importance to the motor caravanner. They have always been a help to the man with limited time, or to the man who does not really enjoy motoring. But the scope they afford for avoiding either the outward or the return drive, and the consequent saving in mileage, is now of significant financial consequence.

If, for example, a van's consumption is 20 miles per gallon, and taking it by Southern Ferries to San Sebastian will avoid 600 miles' travelling one way across France, then the saving will be 30 gallons. Of course the longer journey will be more expensive. But the 600 miles saved will mean 600 miles more to go before the next service, and will represent a further saving to set against the higher ferry fare.

The longer ferry may not necessarily be so much more expensive. Although passengers will almost certainly pay more, and if they take cabins considerably more, than on the short sea routes, the van itself may well pay less. On many of the longer routes, indeed, a van pays less with each accompanying passenger, until with a driver and three passengers it travels completely free. Many passengers regard the thirty-six hours to Northern Spain or Sweden, the forty-eight hours to Lisbon, or the seventy-two hours to Morocco, as a holiday in itself – a 'mini-cruise' as some of the ferry operators promote it.

It can be seen that when private lines are not operating on the same routes as Sealink, comparisons of cost have to take several factors into account. This can apply even on the short sea crossing, where Hoverlloyd operates its 'Channel Fly-over' from Ramsgate to Calais. Here all you pay for is the car; the driver and up to six passengers travel free. A well-filled motor caravan might find this a cheaper alternative to the conventional car ferry (faster too, at only forty minutes).

On the short sea crossings, however, there is one exceptional item in the fare regulations which must be borne in mind. It is the High Vehicle supplement payable on certain sailings by vehicles more than 6 ft 6 in high. This means 'either the height of a vehicle as shown in the manufacturer's specification, or the actual height (including roof-rack and anything loaded on the roof), whichever is the greater'.

Although this regulation applies to more than half the total crossings from Dover to Calais and from Dover to Boulogne in July and August, it is applicable to a very much smaller proportion on the other crossings, even at the height of the season. The flexible motor caravanner can avoid ever travelling on them. He can be grateful that agitation in the motor caravanning press persuaded more and more vans to boycott the useful South-ampton–Cherbourg route, until European Ferries made the High Vehicle supplement selective there too. For during several seasons it applied to all sailings.

This High Vehicle supplement catches all but the smallest of the compact estate-car conversions. On the four Sealink car-ferry routes to Ireland 'Motorized-caravans' are specifically singled out for higher rates than cars when their length exceeds 16 ft 6 in. Although there is no extra charge for height as such, accommodation for high vehicles is restricted and arrangements to ship them must be made in advance.

A recently introduced route to Ireland, which has proved very popular with the French, might also interest motor caravanners on an extended tour of Europe, who wish to enjoy a 'circular tour' of the British Isles without driving right across England twice. This is Normandy Ferries' service from Le Havre to Rosslare. Another good service is the Sheerness-Flushing crossing run by the Olau Line.

There are many useful car ferries elsewhere in Europe, such as those between Denmark and Sweden, and those between Italy and Greece. Amongst the most expensive are those from France to Corsica; amongst the cheapest and most useful that from Algeciras in southern Spain to the Spanish port of Ceuta in North Africa. But all except the smaller fixed-roof motor caravans must be driven between these ferries – from Calais to Nice, or from Boulogne to Brindisi. The extensive Motorail system is useful for smaller motor caravans, but check the width and height regulations, as these vary.

3 Ireland

For the motor caravanner Ireland has all the advantages of Great Britain, whilst sharing only one disadvantage – that of climate. Here *dépaysement* is total. In crossing the Irish sea he immerses himself in another culture just as completely as if crossing the Channel.

It is true that the scenery is in many ways less exciting than in Britain. But it is very different. Here man has acted on the landscape in a quite different way, creating scattered smallholdings instead of nucleated villages. Of the nine members of the enlarged Common Market, only Luxembourg has a smaller population. But if Ireland were peopled with the same density as Luxembourg she would have ten million inhabitants instead of only three million.

Yet before the Great Famine of the mid-nineteenth century her population was eight million. The sense of this larger past accentuates the Celtic, Atlantic melancholy, which the motor caravanner will enjoy as he parks beside deserted cabins, or picnics in the overgrown garden of a roofless country house.

There are plenty of organized sites. There are even more informal ones, run by small farmers. And there are thousands of empty acres for those who require neither.

The unspoilt quality of this motor caravanner's paradise at Britain's back door is best illustrated by the reaction of the rare visitors from the Continent. A Frenchman: 'It is so wonderfully primitive. You feel you have stepped back several centuries, more so than in Brittany or the Morvan.'

A Spanish girl: 'You see poverty in Ireland in a way that no longer exists in Spain. It applies to all classes. Where I was staying our neighbour was a Countess, and used to wander about in an old tweed costume feeding her chickens, in a way no Spanish *condesa* would ever do.'

4 France

France is the best country in the world for motor caravanning. She offers a wide variety of beautiful scenery, the monuments and memories of a rich historical past, a dense network of well-surfaced roads bearing little traffic, and a climate which at every season can offer regions neither too hot nor too cold.

It is not as expensive as is commonly thought. Even petrol,

which for two decades cost more than anywhere else save Portugal, now stands at a higher price in several other countries. And diesel fuel is cheaper than in England. So are other important items: fruit and vegetables, especially when bought from open-air markets; eggs and milk, especially when purchased direct from the farm; yoghourts, pâté, and that very French delicacy chestnut cream, especially when acquired at the vast new out-of-town 'hypermarkets', which also offer petrol at a 3–5% discount.

Cheapest of all are the camp sites. These vary from luxury sites, offering as many amenities as a four-star hotel, to simple municipal *campings,* which charge perhaps a quarter as much. Some villages, as indicated in the chapter on wild camping, may even put a free site at their visitors' disposal. And the whole vast, under-populated land is a standing invitation to the motor caravanner who wishes to simply ignore organized sites altogether.

This invitation is reinforced, surprisingly enough, by the superficially unwelcoming attitude of the inhabitants. I write these words reluctantly, after spending many happy months in France over many years. But I recognize that 'unwelcoming' is the first impression for many newcomers. What they are really describing is indifference. The French are so used to foreigners that they do not press round them with questions, examining their vans, and telling them where to park. They are too interested in their own affairs and their own culture, which they *know* to be superior to anyone else's.

But this indifference has two advantages for the motor caravanner. The first is that he is left to lead his own life, free from interference. No one, helpfully or unhelpfully, will come up with suggestions or criticisms as he draws up on the square by the village church. Nor will he be disturbed by noise. After eight, doors will be locked and shutters closed, as each household withdraws, indifferent to everything outside itself and the French view of the world reflected on the television screen.

The other advantage of their indifference is that he can observe the French as they really are. Over breakfast next morning he can watch the village awakening to life as if he and his van were invisible. The farmer's wife driving a herd of cows out to the fields; the man in *bleus de travail* and beret, smoking a Gauloise cigarette, and calling at the *boulangerie* for a *baguette*; and the *facteur* on his round delivering letters, never give the van or its occupant so much as a glance.

There is an enormous choice of scenery, from the rocky coasts of Brittany to the sophisticated shores of the Côte d'Azur. Because of his instant mobility the motor caravanner can enjoy not only the more obvious delights like these, but also less known and less frequented, though equally beautiful regions.

Behind those Breton fishing villages, for example, lie the quiet farms, clear streams, and deep forests of the Ar-goat, or 'land of the wood', as the Bretons have named it. Only a few miles inland from the teaming Riviera *plages* lie the empty landscapes, the lavender fields, and the decaying hamlets of Haute-Provence.

A journey across France is, of course, what most motor caravanners can look forward to on their way to Spain, Portugal, Morocco, Italy, or several other destinations. Cherbourg to Perpignan does not have to be twenty-four hours of gruelling thunder down *routes nationales*. It can mean a chance to explore Normandy, Perche, Maine, Touraine, Limousin, Périgord, Quercy, Guyenne, Languedoc, and Roussillon.

5 Spain

Spain is the most popular destination for all Britons travelling abroad, amongst whom motor caravanners are no exception. One of the reasons for this popularity is Spain's reputation for being cheap, for in 1950 her government deliberately devalued the peseta in order to encourage tourism. In due course Spain was to have the greatest tourist industry in Europe, including some of the most modern and luxurious camp sites.

But all the imported purchasing power has forced up the price of goods and services. At the height of summer certain areas of Spain are having to import fruit and vegetables from more expansive France. And the concrete ribbon which extends along much of the Spanish Mediterranean has obliterated some of the most exquisite wild camping sites which existed fifteen years ago.

Spain, which in 1950 did not have a single camp site, now has hundreds, including some of the best in Europe. But the amenities they offer have cost money, and the motor caravanner will find them expensive.

However, he need no longer fear that his van's suspension is likely to succumb to the irregularities of the Spanish road surfaces. Even the secondary roads are fast being asphalted. The main routes are now beautifully graded four-lane highways, provided with convenient picnic areas.

But simply because of its geography – those fierce sierras which cut up the flat plains and fertile valleys of the Spanish landscape – the road system is, and will always be, less dense than those of less spectacular lands. All too often this geography dictates that there is only one way to get from A to B. And all too often the lorries hurrying fish from the coast, half the commercial travellers of Bilbao and Barcelona, tourists of every nationality from Norway to New Zealand, and the provincial governor with his outriders and cortège will have decided to travel along it at the same time as your motor caravan.

It is the people as much as the prices that attract visitors to Spain. But even a warm, friendly temperament can have disadvantages. It makes Spain a noisy land. The laughter from the numerous cafés of even the smallest towns continues until the early hours. The beautiful Spanish language is clear and lucid, but it is terribly penetrating, and the voices which speak it are never still. Now that Spain's automobile industry has grown to be the seventh largest in the world, the traffic on her roads seems never to cease. The motor caravanner's nights will here be more disturbed than in lands less obviously *simpático*.

Yet *simpático* will be his enduring impression, from the friendly frontier officials, who joke even as they meticulously search the van for smuggled drugs, to the wineshop proprietor who invites him to 'taste' half a dozen glassfuls before he eventually chooses the barrel from which to refill his bottles.

He can visit some of the most beautiful and quintessentially Spanish regions without driving all the way to Benidorm or Torremolinos. The Pyrenees offer unspoilt valleys with clear, fast rivers and majestic forests, just across the frontier. At the head of many of these valleys the more enterprising of the huddled stone villages have established comfortably equipped camp sites. Naturally, too, there are ample opportunities for wild camping. And following those valleys for a short hour or two downstream will lead him into the other worlds of proud Navarre and sunbaked Aragon.

6 Portugal

Portugal is a country of surprises. Although so near Spain it is a different, gentler, sadder land. With its long Atlantic seaboard it has more rain, but then the countryside is greener. It is too far south to catch the Gulf Stream, so that its vast beaches offer a bracing rather than a sub-tropical swim. The long, falling sounds of its unpronounceable language have enabled its poets to write some of the most sadly evocative verse known to literature. The word *saudade*, expressing this deep nostalgia of the national soul, is in continuous use.

The motor caravanner, crossing one of the eleven frontier posts from Spain, or landing from the car ferry at Lisbon, will be made aware of the gentle sadness by the calm of the Portuguese villages, and by their utter silence at night. He will be reminded of the long association with overseas territories many times larger than the mother country by that exuberant mingling of Gothic with Oriental in the Manueline architecture; by Baroque country churches, which seem to belong to Brazilian landscapes; by meetings with old ladies, who have lived in Goa, and with young men who have served in Angola; by an almost English taste for tea, here called *chá* after the same Indian word that gave the British 'cup of char'.

Many imported items are expensive, so fill up with petrol before you leave Spain, and take on as many bottles of spirits as you are likely to need during your stay. Locally produced foodstuffs are cheap enough, and if you have room, stock up with dried figs at an Algarve market, or with rich red wine at a local *adega cooperativa*.

Sites are few, but of a very high standard. In theory motor caravans are supposed to use them, but the authorities recognize that we have to park somewhere. In some 250 nights in Portugal I only used a site on two occasions, yet was never moved on or otherwise disturbed. And everywhere beautiful drinking fountains, which might have been specially sited for the motor caravanner's convenience, gush sweet spring water.

7 Italy

Britain and Italy share the problems caused by dense population. In both countries this can sometimes raise difficulties for the motor caravanner.

Italian cities, it must be admitted, are more beautiful than English cities. Indeed, it can be argued that with their *piazze* reserved for pedestrians, their vast terrace cafés, and all the open-air life their climate makes possible, they are the only modern cities where urban living can still be a pleasure. But much of that pleasure springs from the quaintness and intimacy of medieval town planning, which leaves little space for parking, or even for manoeuvring any vehicle larger than a Fiat Cinquecento.

The little Fiats proliferate also on the country roads, which are just as twisting as those of Britain, and even narrower. The Fiat company has in fact financed the construction of some of the *autostrade*, the earliest of which were built some thirty years before Britain's first motorway. But they are not free, and their progressive toll bears heavily on larger vehicles such as motor caravans.

The motor caravanner who avoids this expense by taking alternative, ordinary roads, will find himself facing some poor surfaces (such as the route between Naples and Sorrento), and some treacherous drops (as on the coast road from Paestum south towards Calabria). He may feel amply compensated by some of the unspoilt spots where he can draw up, overlapping the blue Tyrrhenian, or overlooked by classical ruins in a Salvator Rosa landscape. But he will never for long be allowed to enjoy these beauties in solitude.

From hard experience I have learned that twenty minutes are the maximum of peace I can hope for in the deepest Appenines or the wildest Abruzzi before the *bambini* descend, fingering the van, engaging me in conversation, begging for *lire*. This constant human interference can often make wild camping disagreeable.

Italy is less well-equipped with organized sites than France. The fees are near to the French maximum, but they are often beautifully situated, and are generally well run. Sites are frequently enclosed, which is a useful precaution, for during her history Italy has been an occupied country for many centuries, and 'Resistance' habits of petty thieving die slowly.

Food, except for bread, fresh fruit, and vegetables, is more expensive than many visitors expect. The climate too has some surprises. Not everyone revels in the high temperatures of the dry, Mediterranean summer. And I recall a continuously wet

May in Umbria, and bitter cold near Naples in January and at Metaponto in March, when the gas froze inside the van.

Despite these drawbacks Italy and the Italians will attract the motor caravanner again and again. Magnificent examples of architecture, from classical ruins to Renaissance churches, are to be found throughout the country. Everywhere the liquid language of Dante and Caruso is spoken and sung by the most stylish race in Europe. If he has once parked at Sorrento at Easter, beside Lake Como in June, or near Asolo in September, he will drive north across the Alps breathing *'a rivederci, Italia'*.

Because of the importance of tourist trade to the economy, the Italian government goes out of its way to help the visitor, issuing petrol coupons at a substantial discount, and offering abundant free handouts of well-produced and helpful descriptive literature in every language.

8 Switzerland

With all its mountains, and its high cost of living, Switzerland would seem a most unsuitable country for motor caravans. However, half of its surface is plain, and not all its highlands are jagged Alps. One sixth Jura, one third Alps, and one half 'Midlands' is how the Swiss themselves divide it up.

Although prices are high, in such a small land one is never far from the frontiers of Italy, France, or Austria, where food-stuffs are less expensive. Even inside Switzerland you will learn, like the Swiss themselves, to bless Mr Migros, whose bulk-buying chain of supermarkets performs miracles of under-cutting. Petrol is so much cheaper here than elsewhere that Swiss Customs actually take special precautions to see that visitors leave with no more in their tanks than they had on entering.

Indeed, I have heard it asserted – though I have yet to put it to the test – that one can live in remote corners of the less-visited cantons, like Uri or Unterwalden, as reasonably as anywhere in Europe. Certainly, while descending through Uri from the St-Gothard Pass, I have noticed many ideal wild camping sites, which I had never expected to find in a purely Alpine setting.

But the motor caravanner's happiest moments of wild camping in Switzerland will be beside the lakes, especially at the smaller resorts and villages. The scene is much the same, whether on

Lake Constance, on the many lakes of German Switzerland, around Lakes Geneva and Neufchatel in French Switzerland, or on the Swiss shores of Lakes Maggiore and Lugano in that delightful combination of Latin warmth and German cleanliness which is Italian Switzerland.

In a quiet, neat little harbour pleasure craft bob up and down only a foot or so below the level of the quay, and the carpark alongside the trim lawns is refreshingly still by comparison with the distant stream of traffic, diverted to a bypass on the other side of the little town. Here, undisturbed, the motor caravanner eats and reads and sleeps, taking on his water at the nearby drinking fountain. If he raises his eyes to the further shore he will see the wooded slopes at Interlaken, or the casino of the comic-opera Italian enclave of Campione d'Italia at Lugano, or the eternal snows of Mont Blanc high above the clouds at Lake Geneva.

Ski-ing and the motor caravan

Winter camping is becoming increasingly popular with both motor and trailer caravanners and many sites now remain open all the year round. The London tourist offices will supply a list – usually free.

In general, caravanners who wish to ski will have to be prepared to motor from the site daily and drive back in the evening. This will rather put the damper on the *aprés-ski* but, if ski-ing is your true love, it will be cheaper from a van than a hotel.

A gas heater, flued to the exterior, would be an asset. Bottled gas may fail to vapourize in extreme cold and it would be wise to have a spare container kept inside the van, or a small portable gas ring with disposable canisters. Regular winter caravanners usually choose propane rather than butane gas, because it vapourizes at lower temperatures.

Of course, the van must be fully insulated and particular attention should be paid to the floor, with felt and carpet inside and expanded polystyrene (or a proprietary product such as ICI's Purlboard) stuck underneath. Windows, if not double glazed, should be covered at night with sheets of foam or polystyrene. *But do ensure there is adequate ventilation.*

Most winter sites have mains electricity hook-ups and some of them are suitable for electric heaters – which solve all prob-

This British family in Switzerland prove that motor caravanning can be enjoyed in any weather. For a long stay above the snowline, however, they would need to provide special insulation for their elevating roof.

lems. But do make sure your van has been wired in accordance with the recommendations of the Institute of Electrical Engineers.

Motoring will pose few problems. Snow clearance is generally more efficient and effective than in Britain. On some mountain roads tyre chains are obligatory. The AA or RAC will supply the necessary information and tell you where chains can be hired.

9 Belgium

On one occasion my mother and I travelled across northern France from St-Malo in Brittany to Ostend. She had not visited the Belgian coast before, and sat stupefied as we drank a cup of tea soon after crossing the frontier.

'If I hadn't experienced it, I would never have thought it possible to move so abruptly from deep French rural peace to this extraordinary atmosphere of buckets and spades and macintoshes and east winds. It reminds me more than anything of the Lincolnshire coast – not Skegness itself, but some of the lesser resorts, like Chapel St Leonards.'

In acknowledging that her judgement was absolutely on target, I am not necessarily ruling out the Belgian beaches for motor caravanners. For that bracing but far from beautiful Lincolnshire coast is where so many Midlanders park their caravans all summer. And behind the dunes of La Panne and Blankenberghe lie better fare and a more colourful hinterland than Sutton on Sea and Mablethorpe can offer. Belgian cuisine is a nice blend of French ingredients with Germanic substantiality. Bruges is very much interesting than Boston.

However, not many motor caravanners will acquire such a taste for the Simenon-like flavour of Flanders, that they will wish to prolong their stay amongst its cobbles and tramways for an entire holiday. After halting at bilingual Brussels, capital of the new Europe, they should continue to the south of French-speaking Wallonie. Here the densely populated lowlands give way to the deserted, hilly Ardennes, as peaceful an area as anywhere in Europe.

10 Holland

The motor caravanner arriving in Holland must adjust his scale of measurement if he is to get the best out of his visit. Fortunately this comes almost automatically. For the horizon moves into the distance as he drives under the vast sky, already known to him from the Dutch landscape painters.

This adjustment once made, the journey from one former port to another along the now landlocked Zuider Zee becomes apparently as long as from province to province in a larger land. And the differences between urbanized Noord-Holland and pastoral Friesland across the Afsluitdijk, or between the heaths of Drente and the green hills of Limburg in the far south, further magnify the illusion of distance.

The Dutch are great tent-campers, and manufacture some cunning tent-trailers to tow behind their ingenious little Dafs. There are organized sites in plenty, including some conveniently situated for visiting the world-famous museums of the Hague and of beautiful, canal-ringed Amsterdam. But urban wild camping in these and other cities of seventeenth-century origin would be difficult.

Although the Dutch are not great motor caravanners themselves, the area round Amsterdam International airport is
Europe's biggest market for second-hand vans, especially for
the more primitive, fixed-roof, home-made conversions. This
market developed because Amsterdam is the favourite airport
of arrival for charter flights from North America, and returning
Americans often needed to sell their vans after their tour of
Europe. Although there are now plenty of established dealers,
you can still pick up a bargain by studying the prices scrawled
by their owners on the clapped-out VW kombis waiting in and
near the Dam.

11 West Germany

Much of the scenery of the middle Rhine or of the Bavarian
Alps is astonishingly romantic. The longest of her main routes
apart from the *autobahnen* is the beautiful and aptly named
Romantische Strasse. And the motor caravanner will find the
Black Forest, the Moselle valley and the Saxon plain as different
from each other as when the Grand Duke of Baden, the Arch-
bishop of Trier, and the Elector of Hannover were still independent princes of the Holy Roman Empire.

Of course it is ruinously expensive. For every single one of the
dozen or so currency adjustments since 1948 has been against
us. But unlike France and Italy, the autobahns in Germany are
free. The motor caravanner will find himself using them not
only to travel fast, but for the convenience of their rest-places,
which will save him the fees of organized sites. Many of the old
two-lane motorways, which cut through beautiful fir forests, are
now being widened. So despite the expensive food and petrol,
the motor caravanner can console himself with the fact that the
cost of any more conventional holiday in Germany would be
prohibitive.

12 Austria

Alps cover a greater area of Austria than of Switzerland. In its
three most visited and most mountainous provinces – Vorarlberg,
Tyrol and Salzburg – there is often very little room for a motor
caravan. Even the main roads are narrow, and in constant use
by tractors belonging to local farmers. Carparks are few and
far between, and sites tend to be small and crowded, so that a

visit to a long valley like the Zillertal can be a frustrating experience.

Vienna itself is not a bad city for urban wild camping. But the motor caravanner's happiest memories may be of the relatively tourist-free Danube valley, and of the almost totally unvisited Waldviertel and Mühlviertel between there and the Czech frontier.

The less interesting Neusiedler See on the Hungarian frontier belongs geographically to the flat Hungarian plain: it is the weekend retreat of Viennese caravanners. The lakes of Carinthia in the south are both warmer, and more dramatic in their setting.

13 Denmark

When I visited the extreme north-west of Jutland, the inhabitants confirmed that they could converse in their local dialect with people from the coast of Northumberland, so that standard English, too, came easily to them. In fact the Danes are in a good many ways like the people of Northern England, where many of them settled a thousand years ago. They have the same qualities of kindness beneath a deep reserve. It was only in our third day as the sole GB on a crowded camp site that anyone spoke to us. But as we drove out on the morning of the fourth it was to an impromptu chorus of cheers and clapping.

The motor caravanner may not wish to linger for long on the flat east coast, with its cold, pounding seas, but he will be amply compensated by the lakes of north and central Jutland, and the idyllic farmland of the southern islands – Funen, Langeland, Laaland and Falster. Because of the number of bridges, it costs a motor caravan no more to travel from Jutland to Copenhagen by this route than by the better known direct ferry across the 'Big Belt', thus visiting seven islands instead of only two.

14 Sweden

Sweden is the fourth largest country in Europe after Russia, France and Spain. Yet it is a pleasure to drive across, for its well-engineered roads traverse attractive, undulating countryside without mountainous extremes. Its capital is a very beautiful modern city. And surprisingly its many internal car ferries are free.

Its reputation for being expensive, however, is all too justified. There are no cheap little restaurants off the beaten track such as France still offers. So stock up before you land at Gothenburg or Halsingborg.

15 Norway

The friendly Norwegians are few on the ground, clinging literally to the edge of their dramatic, narrow land. For human settlement on the long fjords is limited to a thin strip between high-tide level and the steep slopes behind.

The combination of mountainous country, the long winters, and the scattered population means that not all of the narrow, switchback roads are properly surfaced. Even some of the main highways which cross the deserted plateaux are merely tracks of hard earth. But wherever there is room, wild camping can be enjoyed as nowhere else.

16 Finland

Unless you are prepared to do the long hard drive through Lapland, your route to Finland will be by sea from Sweden. The ferries call at the autonomous Aland Islands, which are Swedish-speaking but under Finnish sovereignty. No charge is made for a break of journey in this quiet northern archipelago, which is well suited for motor caravanning.

Situated on the edge of Russia and in the penumbra of the Arctic, Finland's landscape seems to be made up entirely of birch forests and lakes. This may sound like a recipe for unending beauty, but it can prove somewhat monotonous, although the motor caravanner in search of a peaceful holiday will find it here amongst the quiet, friendly people.

17 Yugoslavia

Wild camping is discouraged in Yugoslavia. Although I have not been disturbed myself, I have heard numerous stories of motor caravanners 'moved on', ordered to go to organized sites, or subjected to upsetting questioning. However, the Istrian and Dalmatian coasts are not only beautiful, but much of the area is completely undeveloped.

The general atmosphere is curiously ambivalent. Does the country belong to East or West? Is it in central Europe or in

southern Europe? Is it wholly European at all, or at least partly
Asiatic? How much residual Latinity survives amongst these
South Slavs? And can their attitude rightly be described as
friendly? The motor caravanner better than most has a chance
of answering these questions.

18 Greece

The two main drawbacks are the high price of petrol, and the
difficulty of taking a motor caravan to all but a handful of the
lovely Greek isles, although Crete, Euboea and Corfu can be
reached easily enough.

It is a long journey actually to get there, both east and south,
but once you arrive, there are some idyllic spots for camping
wild. There are now a dozen or so Government-owned sites
with good facilities, and in perfect positions along the coast.

The Greek people are both friendly and open, and you will be
able to eat cheaply in tavernas and bars. Fruit, vegetables and
fish are cheap and plentiful in season, and local wine, as well as
retsina and ouzo, are inexpensive.

The rugged coastline of Greece offers the motor caravanner ideal spots for
wild camping.

19 Turkey

Istanbul is a great meeting point for motor caravanners, before they travel eastwards into Asia. Do not miss the opportunity of seeing this beautiful city, and visiting Saint Sophia, the Topkapi Serai, the Blue Mosque, and the Byzantine ramparts. But listen carefully to the stories of anyone returning from a journey east. Although you should not get too alarmed by them, you may pick up tips which will be of use to you once you have crossed the wonderful new Bosporus bridge into Asia.

For there are certain roads where travellers have been robbed, and certain whole areas best avoided. And there is nothing like up-to-date and first-hand information to tell you which. Even in safer regions many motor caravanners prefer to use the excellent chain of motel-camp sites attached to BP service stations.

By listening you will also learn where you can park safely. I know one motor caravanner in his mid-seventies who returns each spring to camp wild, unprotected and accompanied only by his wife, on the glorious Cilician coast opposite Cyprus. But he has struck up a friendship with the local chief of police!

20 Eastern Europe

Having never crossed the Iron Curtain myself, I can only pass on the information I have had from motor caravanners returning from Eastern Europe, and all comment unfavourably on two features.

One is the obligation to exchange several pounds for each day's stay in a country. This is far more than they need to live on, and forces them to throw money away on meals in luxury restaurants, and on inferior, unwanted souvenirs.

The other is the monotony of the human landscape. For however much we rail against the consumer society and its waste, we sadly miss the competitive High Streets, the exciting department stores, and the stimulating variety of village inns and country restaurants.

Wild camping, possible in some of these countries, is definitely frowned on in Russia itself, where the motor caravanner, like everyone else, must keep to his itinerary. Opportunities for personal contact vary in the same way, from a maximum amongst the friendly Poles to a minimum in the Soviet.

On the other hand there have been some remarkable breakthroughs on every level by enterprising motor caravanners operating in the further reaches of the USSR. Mr Alan Johnston, who drove his wife and three children round the world in a Commer Highwayman between 1965 and 1968, was even able to persuade the Soviet and Iranian authorities to allow him to drive across a long-closed frontier bridge after his exploration of the Russian Caucasus.

21 Asia

Again, I have no personal experience of *les chemins de Katmandu*, the route which has been opened up from Istanbul across Turkey, Persia, Afghanistan and Pakistan to India and beyond. But if Dervla Murphy managed it more than ten years ago on her bicycle,* it cannot present insuperable obstacles to motor caravans, especially as much of it is now asphalted.

In Persia petrol at least is cheap, but travellers have recently been put off by the bond (of the vehicle's value when new), which must be deposited while it remains within the country. For a time ADAC were prepared for a modest fee to supply a document to replace this. But at the time of writing I understand that this facility has been withdrawn. Anyone planning a long overland journey must check on this and the many other formalities to be encountered, as these change not only from year to year but sometimes from month to month.

In Persia, too, as in Turkey and Afghanistan, those who camp wild away from other travellers risk very real dangers.

In India the dangers arise from attempting to negotiate the crowded, narrow highways, where peasants and their carts have little road sense, and where sacred cows have none at all. Progress beyond India is complicated by the difficulty of getting visas to cross self-isolated Burma, by war-ravaged Vietnam, and by that ultimate denial of the motor caravanning ethos, Mao's China.

Those who have shipped their vans to Japan find this land too unsatisfactory for travelling. The one quarter of the land which is not mountainous is so densely populated that there is often nowhere for a van to park. And the Japanese economic miracle has been unbalanced. Concentration has been on

* *Full Tilt* by Dervla Murphy (John Murray).

industrial rather than social investment, and much of the road system is still medieval.

The Nearer East, on the other hand, has made an unexpectedly favourable impression on many motor caravanners. It is perhaps not so surprising that they have spent happy months at the well-run site at Beirut, capital of the Lebanon, or swimming and sun-bathing at winter-free Eilat, Israel's port on the Red Sea. But I have heard equally good reports from an enterprising couple who spent many weeks parked in Kuwait. They even received every courtesy from that dreaded body, the Iraqi police, on their way there.

The moral is that everything depends on your attitude, and on approaching a country in the right way. So listen carefully but with a pinch of salt, to the tales of all those returned travellers at Istanbul.

22 North Africa

The best country in North Africa for the motor caravanner is undoubtedly Morocco. It is the easiest to reach, by the short, cheap ferry from Algeciras to Ceuta. It has done more to encourage tourists, and also has more to offer them.

When in 1912 the greater part of the country became a protectorate of the French, it was modernized, and given the best road network in Africa. But the French did nothing to disturb its ancient traditions. Even their fine new towns were built at some distance from the ancient Moroccan cities, whose narrow streets, crowded with figures in native costume, have survived intact from the Middle Ages.

It is also the richest country in North Africa. For instead of being confined to a coastal belt between the Mediterranean and the desert, it has a long Atlantic shore, and the great Atlas mountain ranges ensure an ample rainfall. The Atlantic always brings milder winter weather than the Mediterranean, and the Atlas shelters the extreme south from the cold winds from Europe. The coast near Agadir is one of the great gathering places for motor caravanners avoiding the coldest months. They enjoy not only the sun, the swimming and the surfing, but the cheap and delicious fruit and vegetables from the nearby fertile valleys.

In Algeria state socialism makes it a less attractive place to visit. It is also rather more expensive; and this cost is compounded by the Algerian motor insurance, which motor caravanners are obliged to take out at the frontier (the Green Card not being accepted). But some prefer the Algerian oases to those of the Moroccan Sahara.

Everyone likes Tunisia and the Tunisians. But as the most westernized country of North Africa it is less colourful. Libya, under its present puritan Islamic leadership, is uncongenial to many visitors, and no longer provides the advantage of membership of the sterling area.

Egypt is anxious to encourage tourists, and has plenty to show them. To its ten thousand years of history, with the monuments these have left behind, it adds surprising success in the fight against inflation. A few well-guarded camp sites beside the Red Sea and on the banks of the Nile, and this would be an ideal place for the motor caravanner. Even as things are, I have met some who cannot speak too highly of their stay there. But they were cautious people who knew how to keep a careful eye on their possessions.

Right at the other end of North Africa another, unexpected motor caravanners' paradise exists in the Canary Islands. This Spanish province lies on the latitude of the extreme south of Morocco. With free-port status the islands offer Spanish wine and foods as cheaply as in Spain, New Zealand butter and Argentine tinned meat as cheaply as in England, petrol cheaper than anywhere outside the Middle East, and Scotch whisky cheaper than anywhere on earth. They also offer their own fresh fruit and vegetables, spectacular scenery and year-round sun, but a certain exposure to wind. At a surprisingly reasonable cost motor caravanners can travel with their vans aboard direct from England, from Barcelona, from Malaga and from Cadiz.

23 Central and Southern Africa

From the Cape to Cairo, or at least from the more attainable Ceuta to Cairo, is many a motor caravanner's dream. But he would be unwise to attempt it in anything other than either a vehicle with four-wheel drive, or one of the very lightest conversions. Coachbuilt vans are too heavy and insufficiently powerful to risk getting bogged down in sand or mud.

I have met plenty of travellers who have crossed the Sahara by one of the well-used routes, but their more serious difficulties have come later. These can include problems with visas and other formalities involved in crossing the numerous frontiers which have split up West and Equatorial Africa since Independence, as well as floods and bad road conditions which are to be expected when negotiating the rivers and tropical forests of this exotic region. But they are not insuperable, for I have met a Landrover arriving from the Ivory Coast, Renault 4Ls from Kenya via the Congo, and even a 2 cv Citroën from Dahomey.

There are perfectly practicable routes from Equatorial through to Southern Africa, in particular through Tanzania and Zambia. Enquiries must, of course, be made on the spot in order to avoid areas of uncertain security.

Once in the Republic of South Africa, to which motor caravans can of course be shipped directly, climatic and road conditions approximate to Europe. It has almost 500 organized 'caravan parks', but I know motor caravanners who camp wild on the coast of Cape Province. However, I would advise readers to enquire very carefully locally before following their example.

24 North America

Whether on the landscaped freeways, or in the camping areas deep in the great National Parks, the motor caravanner may well feel dwarfed when confronted by smart pick-up 'campers', and by the massive motor homes of Dodge and Winnebago. Here the 'RecV' is right in the centre of the burgeoning leisure industry.

Site fees, especially for one person alone driving a van, are more than Europeans are accustomed to pay. But little else is, for our own inflation rate has brought us up to the once relatively high transatlantic price levels. Food is approximately the same price as in Britain. Petrol, even after the shock of the energy crisis, remains substantially cheaper.

However, the high wage structure makes all services expensive. This includes anything in the way of motor repairs, which is one reason for not taking one's own van. Others include the formalities, such as the nasty-sounding 'steam spraying', involved in landing any vehicle in the United States.

One alternative is to use a 'fly-drive' scheme which provides a motor caravan as part of the package. A second alternative would be to arrange an exchange with an American or Canadian motor caravanner who wants to see Europe. At the time of writing a 'Register' for would-be exchangers, though often mooted, does not exist. But offers appear from time to time in the correspondence columns and amongst the small advertisements of the motor caravanning press. Similarly, a letter written to one of the North American open-air journals might provide results for anyone hoping to make an exchange.

The following list of American magazines may prove useful:
Better Camping, 1027 North Seventh Street, Milwaukee, Wisconsin 53233
Camping and Trailering Guide, Rt 1, Box 780, Quincy, California 95971
Trailer Life, 23495 Craftsman Road, Calabasas, California 91302
Woodalls Trailer Travel, 500 Hyacinth Place, Highland Park, Illinois 60035

25 Latin America
Mexico is easy to reach from the States, and is very much cheaper. In certain ways it also offers a more European 'feel', with more emphasis on the quality of life than on the standard of living. But here, as in all parts of Latin America, you should be extremely careful about camping wild, even though in many places there is no alternative. There are exceptions to this general rule. The countryfolk of Guatemala are as honest as they are unsophisticated.

Costa Rica continues to live up to its reputation as the Switzerland of Central America. But make quite sure of the local situation before you expose yourself to robbery, kidnapping, or plain murder. Remember that in certain countries, including Colombia and Venezuela, little-publicized guerilla groups operate in the interior to make life additionally unsafe.

The Pan-American Highway, which will one day enable motor caravanners to drive all the way from Alaska to the southern tip of Patagonia, is broken between Panama and Colombia by the thick jungle of the 'Darien gap'. Thereafter road conditions vary widely, from excellent in Argentina to atrocious in Bolivia.

A large number of the Latin American republics are in the dollar area. Even in the others the visitor will find it more convenient to carry travellers' cheques in dollars.

26 Australia and New Zealand

Both Australia and New Zealand have much to offer motor caravanners. Cheap food of excellent quality is available everywhere. Wild camping is safe, and second nature to the inhabitants themselves. Queensland and its Northern Territories in Australia, and to a lesser extent the Northland beyond Auckland in New Zealand, provide a refuge for motor caravanners caught there in winter.

Australia, producing 70% of its oil requirements, has kept petrol at well below European prices. But fit mosquito netting to all windows, doors and rooflights before you set off. For you will find out about Australian flies when you arrive!

Motor caravans are not only known in these lands, but valued. Because of heavy import duties they cost considerably more there than in Britain. As a result there is much loose talk about the possibility of shipping a van out, touring round for a few months, and then selling it at a profit to pay for the trip. It is not quite as easy as that. Regulations are strict, and liable to change. Check them in detail before you make any decision.

Getting further information

This chapter has been an attempt to indicate to the motor caravanner, as opposed to other travellers, what is likely to be his general impression of certain countries and regions. The nearest place for him to acquire more detailed information is his public library. For the up-to-date position regarding visa and health requirements, if any, and for quite remarkable supplies of free literature, he should contact the national tourist offices of the countries that he intends to visit.

The motor caravanner may find the following addresses useful:

The Automobile Association Fanum House, Leicester Square, London wc2
Caravan Abroad Ltd Betchworth, Surrey, RH3 7HS
European Ferries Ltd 4th Floor, Trafalgar House, 11 Waterloo Place, London sw1
Globetrotters' Club BCM/Roving, London wc1v 6xx
Olau-Line Ferry Terminal Building, Sheerness Docks, Kent
The Royal Automobile Club 89–91 Pall Mall, London sw1
Sealink Car Ferry Centre 52 Grosvenor Gardens, London sw1

19 Over sixty years of development

Of course, homes on wheels existed long before the twentieth century. But it was the invention of the internal combustion engine that made possible the combination in one unit of a home on wheels and its means of propulsion. Yet it was more than sixty years after the earliest motor cars that motor caravans appeared in regular production, as opposed to individual conversions.

There were a number of such prototypes. It is even argued that some appeared before trailer caravans designed for towing behind cars. Eccles, still a well-known brand name of Caravans International, made motor caravans before they switched to trailers. One of their early models, built in 1913, had an open front with a folding cab, and very fine seats. When the firm became a company in 1919, it was registered as Eccles Motor Caravans Ltd.

During the 20s a number of the classic makes from the early days of motoring were individually converted into motor caravans. In about 1926, for example, a Model T Ford was given luxurious treatment, which made it a forerunner of later coach-built models. Also in the 20s Lady Diana Cooper and her husband travelled down to south-west France in what she described as a 'cheap little machine', which, however, 'boasted a Rolls Royce bonnet'. It must have borne some resemblance to the compact estate-car conversions of today.

What most of these early conversions had in common was good craftsmanship. Anyone who has lived in, or even briefly examined a pre-war Cheltenham or Eccles will know what skilful joinery and ingenious design went into those durable models, even if by today's standards they seem a little heavy.

Lightness, indeed, became a primary aim of the industry after the Second World War, when new techniques and new materials developed by aircraft manufacturers were adopted. This further emphasized the differences between the 'mobile home' and the

The first Eccles motor caravan, built in Birmingham by W. A. J. Riley, founder of the company, in 1913. Riley took the rear seats off his 1909 Talbot touring car and replaced them with a light caravan body.

A Morris-based Eccles motor caravan, fitted with very small windows.

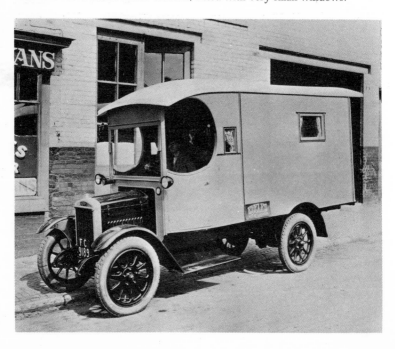

touring van. The mobile home was intended to be almost permanently static. Sometimes they were built within the overall 22 ft limit for towing on public highways. More frequently they were longer, and could only be moved across country by special conveyance. The small wheels were simply for manoeuvring into position on the site.

The touring van, on the other hand, used lighter woods for the frame, thinner aluminium sheeting for the outer panels, glass-fibre wool for the insulation, chipboard and Formica for much of the furniture, plastic for many of the fittings, and foam rubber, to be later superseded by plastic foam, in place of the pre-war flock and interior-sprung mattresses. Previously un-heard-of ratios of length to weight also became possible.

But lightweight materials have lower stress limits, and walls cannot support very many shelves or cupboards. Where they are fitted, they must not be piled too high with books or other heavy objects. Nor must the lockers under the beds be over-loaded, or the van will not tour smoothly.

Yet however powerful the car, and however light and stream-lined the trailer van, together they constitute an articulated vehicle. The caravanner is travelling not on four wheels, but on six. And however convenient a trailer caravan may be, you cannot reach it or use it when in motion; you cannot sleep in it until the four corner jacks have been wound down; you cannot even enter it without stepping into the open.

These disadvantages have been examined in greater detail elsewhere. They must have been present in many different minds during the 50s, but there had to be an individual to make the breakthrough. The man who launched the motor caravanning revolution was an Austrian refugee named Peter Pitt. He believed that a motor caravan should provide not only the manoeuvrability of a car, but its legal and fiscal advantages too. It should be taxed as a car, and subject to the same speed limits, despite its commercial vehicle origins. On the other hand, it should also share the tax as well as the practical advantages of a caravan. It should thus be exempted from purchase tax so long as it conformed to the Customs and Excise Rules, which then demanded fixed standards of facilities for cooking and washing, and of storage for clothes and water.

The advantages of having it both ways could only be gained by a change in interpretation of the law. This would require a test case in the courts. Peter Pitt realized that this might also gain nationwide publicity for what he christened his 'Moto-Caravan'. In 1958 he drove his 1957 prototype, a VW, round the Royal Parks at Windsor, in which commercial vehicles are not allowed. As he hoped, he was prosecuted by the police.

He won his case, not without some difficult moments, but from then on a motor caravan could travel at normal road speeds, yet like a caravan was exempt from purchase tax. The Pitt Moto-Caravan became the first model in regular production.

By 1960 he was offering his conversion not only on the Volkswagen, but also on the Austin 152, the Ford Thames, and the Commer 1500. The layout of beds and seating, which he claimed could be arranged in over thirty different ways, included twin single or double beds in the body of the van, with extra sleeping accommodation for children in the driving cab, or over the engine in the VW. In that year he added to these fixed-roof models one with an elevating sunshine roof.

Others were quick to follow his lead. One firm in particular had been moving in that direction for some years. The firm of Martin Walter had been founded at Folkestone in 1774. Originally harness makers, they specialized in carriage building during the nineteenth century, and coachbuilt special bodies for motor vehicles in the twentieth. They therefore inherited a full measure of that English tradition of good craftsmanship.

Folkestone is not only a resort, but also the English terminus of the cross-channel ferry to Boulogne. One of Martin Walter's directors, a Mr Spencer Apps, noticed, as he took his daily walk, the number of vans which were being used to sleep in on summer evenings, often parked near the quay, so that their owners could catch the first steamer across in the morning.

He realized that there would be a market for such vehicles, if properly designed by a specialist coachbuilding firm such as his own and provided with sleeping arrangements. And thus it was that in 1952 Martin Walter launched on the market a Bedford CA short wheel-base fitted with beds. It was one of his fellow directors, a classical scholar by the name of Lyne-Smith, who found the appropriate Latin-derived name for it: Dormobile.

To the motor caravanner of today the early Dormobiles show much evidence of their automobile ancestry, and they were,

This 1969 Dormobile, on a Bedford CA and with the characteristic
'pramhood' elevating roof, differs very little from its predecessors.

as their well-chosen name implies, cars for sleeping in rather
than for living in. In their early models the beds were not
particularly comfortable. They were formed by folding down the
backs of the hard, narrow, front and rear seats, an ingenious
system devised by Martin Walter, which over the years has
been greatly improved.

However, what mattered was that a motor caravan, a home on
four wheels instead of six, had been designed not by an isolated
individual, but by a manufacturer with sufficient capital and the
marketing ability to launch it into large-scale production. The
marketing flair shows not least in the name. Even today
'dormobile' is in many minds a synonym for motor caravan,
instead of the Martin Walter trademark.

At an early stage the Dormobile acquired a feature even more
famous than the seat conversion. This was the characteristic
elevating roof, operating on a pram-hood system, and placed into

position from inside the vehicle in a single movement. Again, Martin Walter was first in the field.

The van chosen for these early Dormobile conversions was the Vauxhall Bedford CA, with only three gears on its 1594 cc engine. Unlike most other forward-control vans, it did have a small bonnet. This gave the steering at least something of the reassuring feel of a saloon car.

Compactness and manoeuvrability are two of the advantages of a motor caravan over a trailer. A third advantage as indicated earlier, is that stronger and more rigid materials can be used in its construction. For its maximum weight limit is not dependent on how much the car can safely tow, but on how much the van can safely carry. No allowance need be made for heavy steel chassis, towbar, and wheels. The walls can bear as many shelves or cupboards, within reason, as desired, and these can be stowed with as many books or tins as there is room for. There is no need, either, to worry about the effect on towing before filling up the lockers beneath the seats and beds, or before designing an 'end' rather than a 'side' kitchen.

The space for such facilities is, of course, limited by the dimensions of the van as supplied by the manufacturer. In a typical case, that of the BLMC J4, these were 7 ft 11 in long × 5 ft 3 in wide × 4 ft 5 in high. Besides limiting total space available to barely 180 cubic ft, this is a foot too narrow for a bed to fit across the vehicle. Sleeping places are effectively reduced to two.

Obviously one way of breaking out of this 'shell' is by purchasing not a ready-made van, but its cab and chassis alone, and then erecting a 'shell' of one's own on the back. And who better to erect such a shell than a caravan manufacturer, already skilled in building just such living units. Indeed, the idea of placing a trailer caravan shell on the chassis of a commercial van was one which was tried out on a number of motor caravan prototypes.

The first caravan manufacturer to put this into practice was the well-known firm Bluebird Caravans Ltd, now grouped with Sprite, Eccles and Fairholme into Caravans International. The Bluebird Highwayman's exterior appearance showed its debt to the firm's experience in producing gown-vans for clothing retailers and mobile shops. As an owner of one of the earliest I

The Highwayman, longest-lived of all coachbuilt models, by Bluebird (later merged with CI Autohomes). This version on a BMC Morris J2 dates from 1965; by then the Commer 1500 was more frequently used for conversion.

was often asked – and not always as a joke – whether I had any ice cream for sale.

However, many of the permanent basic features of this model were already present. The settee/double bed down one side faced the wardrobe and kitchen unit down the other. An upper hammock could be unfolded above the single bed across the van amidships. The roof light, at that time fixed and providing no ventilation, was bigger than in current models. Over the years it has been reduced in size and the windows have been enlarged. With its ample cupboard and locker space, with sufficient room to stand and to move around, the early Highwayman already exemplified all the essentials of a coachbuilt motor caravan.

But it was somewhat austere, with its plain deal woodwork, in its fittings, and in the box-like appearance. Using the same BMC J2 chassis, with its 1489cc engine, a Bradford firm launched the more luxurious Paralanian. For nearly half as much again in price (£1,250 in 1962 against £878 for the Highwayman) this offered a more attractive interior with pleasing woodwork, a toilet cubicle separate from the wardrobe, and living quarters which could be divided off from the driving cab, with a rounded more caravan-like outline.

The toilet and extra working surfaces had to be paid for in terms of space as well as money. There was only room for two people in the double bed/dinette. And that distinctive curving roof proved to be a regressive development, followed by few motor caravan models since.

Moreover, the Paralanian did nothing to modify the 'corridor' plan, which was the disadvantage of the Highwayman. The earliest departure from this, which was already being advertised in 1960, was the Hadrian. This had a side door which opened into a sitting area, and was one of the few models with an end-kitchen. The Cotswold 'C', launched in 1964 by the West Country coachbuilders Kingscote and Stephens, had a particularly ingenious side-door layout, with rear dinette enjoying all-round vision, and quality joinery and materials. Like the other three early 'purpose-built' vans it was based on the well-tried BMC J2 (though Hadrian also used Commers, Fords and Bedfords).

But these coachbuilt vans were conspicuous in the early 60s more by their size and novel appearance than by their numbers. The converted commercial van was being registered in ever greater quantities. Martin Walter produced several upgraded versions of the original Dormobile. Bluebird started to market their elevating-roof Moto-Plus alongside the Highwayman in 1962.

By the mid-60s the monopoly of the Bedford CA and the BMC J2 had been broken. The Ford Thames, superseded since by the Transit, and the Standard Atlas were two vans which were the bases for several conversions. And for the first time a major motor manufacturer, Rootes, undertook the conversion of its own product in the Commer 'Commer'.

This obvious enthusiasm for and understanding of the motor caravan (significantly lacking at that time in BMC) was only one reason for the rise in popularity of the Commer 1500 amongst converters. The controls, the easy steering, and the independent front suspension put it into a different class from the vans of the 50s. Its advantages were not only mechanical. The slight bulge in its sides gave it, at just the right 12–15 in from the floor, the

The classic Auto-Sleeper conversion of the Commer 1500.

necessary 6 ft of width to accommodate transverse beds.

But of the many firms – Bluebird included from 1961 – who were soon working on Commers, none tailored their conversion more neatly to the vehicle than Auto-Sleeper. Its plan might seem unadventurous, with its dinette/double bed immediately behind the cab, and its cupboards, sink, cooker and wardrobe along the sides. But the very fact that this layout is followed by so many vans, fixed roof, elevating roof and coachbuilt alike, shows its perennial appeal. Auto-Sleeper soon gained a reputation for their careful attention to details – a rounded corner here, a specially strong hinge on some crucial door there.

In recent years the Auto-Sleeper has been adapted to the new generation of vans introduced by Bedford and Leyland. The layout remains almost identical, and improvements are not always immediately apparent. The roof, for example, has not changed in concept, but it is now insulated. The dinette/double bed now converts to front-facing seats for the rear passengers when travelling. For quality as well as conservatism it remains in a class by itself.

When the Auto-Sleeper first came on the roads in the early

60s, it was just one of many conversions carried out by relatively small manufacturers. Some were subsidiaries of bigger concerns, who later preferred to concentrate their activities elsewhere; others were taken over by another converter. All too often the talent for coachbuilding and for carpentry was not allied to the necessary business sense for commercial success, and many of the smaller converters soon went out of business. The following list of names should bring back some memories: Airborne, Bedmobile, Calthorpe (with that unforgettable projecting lantern roof, which featured in so many early cartoons of the motor caravanning life), Caraversions (with its Hitop and its Lotop), Fairthorpe (with its Caravilla), Kenex (with its Carefree), Locomotors (with its Space Traveller), Moortown, Nomad, Pegasus.

This obituary column is not inserted in order to suggest that there is no place for the smaller, and above all for the quality-conscious converter. Cotswold and Auto-Sleeper prove the contrary. But these firms are large enough to have their separate, consumer-orientated sales departments. And it was from the sales end that the next big developments in motor caravanning were to come.

One day in 1959 Peter Duff, managing director of an East London garage, was intrigued by an unusual box-shaped vehicle parked in a layby on the road to Southend. On learning that it was called a Bluebird Highwayman, he wrote to the firm, and was given their agency to market it throughout the Metropolitan London area.

His success in increasing sales was rewarded by the extension of his franchise to the southern half of England in 1961, to the entire United Kingdom in 1963, and to the USA as well in 1964. In this year Bluebird was taken over by the rapidly expanding group of Caravans International, which viewed with misgiving such dynamic marketing flair operating in their favour but outside their organization. So in 1965, when Peter Duff brought back an order from America for no less than 2,800 units, worth eleven million dollars, they commenced negotiations for the acquisition of his firm.

The absorption of Crofton Garages by Caravans International (Motorised), with Peter Duff as Managing Director, meant that for the first time in the industry a marketing man was responsible for the entire product. Henceforward CI intelligently attempted, with every manufacturer's model used, to cater for both sections of the market – the luxury coachbuilt, and the dual-purpose van conversion. The coachbuilt Bedford Bedouin was partnered by the dual-purpose Brigand, the luxury Ford Transit Motorhome by the Wayfarer, just as the Highwayman itself had already been joined by a smaller model, the Wanderer. And although the Sprite Motorhome of 1966 was criticized for being impractical and the Highwayman for becoming more expensive, the number of vans sold proved the venture to be a success.

In CI Autohomes' Autohome on the Ford Transit the luton above the cab was arranged as an upstairs bedroom, lit by a long oval 'Cyclops eye'. The successor to this model is now named the Motorhome.

In the United States the Highwayman, rechristened the Sunbeam Funwagon, achieved a breakthrough which was only halted by the introduction of anti-pollution laws in the later 60s. The novel Autohome, with an 'upstairs bedroom' above the cab, lit by a long oval 'Cyclops eye' in front, followed CI's green Sprites all over the Continent. It was first exhibited at the Paris Motor Show in 1971, and CI have since developed a substantial European export market.

The structure of the Autohome is also novel. Although not a readily detachable 'pickaback', it is built independently of, rather than on to the chassis. It is conceived as a box to move around the world and place on a chassis anywhere – on a Ford chassis in Germany, say, or on a General Motors chassis in America. It can thus sidestep motor import quotas – or anti-pollution laws. The concept's success is shown by the fact that the firm has produced a second, larger model: the Travelhome.

An older and more flamboyant sales personality, who also moved right into the forefront in the same period, never became involved with production. Leslie Wilson, a motorcycle champion of the 20s, inherited a family garage in Brixton, South London. Like Peter Duff, he at once recognized the future ahead of motor caravans. But instead of linking himself with any one manufacturer, he stocked and ordered whatever models his customers wanted. As a result he found himself selling, not any particular motor caravan as such, but the very idea of motor caravanning. To do so he brought into play all the techniques not merely of a salesman, but of a born showman. There was not a camping or caravan exhibition in the 60s without a prominent stand presided over by that short, genial figure, only too happy to explain the workings and advantages of his models on show.

The success of Leslie Wilson's techniques meant expansion. Branches were opened at Bradford (1966), at Epsom (1970) and at Castle Donington near Leicester (1972). Overseas advertising publicity – touring Australia in a Highwayman, for example – sold motor caravanning as the cheapest and most comfortable way of seeing Europe.

The only conversion Wilsons ever carried out themselves was the Adventurer, a giant twice the size of any other British van of the time, based on the Commer $1\frac{1}{2}$ ton LWB Walk Thru', which in 1964 retailed at the then giant price of £3,000 and upwards. Only a few were ever produced. But Wilsons' penchant for size was again revealed in the early 70s, when they began to import the enormous American motor-homes.

The British industry has not scaled such heights – or committed such excesses. But there was a noticeable tendency to 'trade up' by the bigger manufacturers who in the late 60s inherited a large part of a fast-expanding market from the smaller, sometimes amateurish converters of the earlier years of the decade. Developments at CI Autohomes, as they were rechristened in 1972, have already been outlined. The professional Roadranger, by the fine old coachbuilders Jennings of Sandbach, and the well-finished Tourstar by the inheritor of the Paralanian team of craftsmen, illustrated the same tendency. Most significantly of all, Martin Walter introduced their first coachbuilt van. The Debonair continued to use the Bedford chassis – the CA from 1964 and the CF from 1969. The entire body was made of glass fibre, except for the short bonnet, and inside the area was divided into two rooms.

Martin Walter was also amongst the initiators of a quite different development: the mini motor caravan. There had been an earlier attempt to launch this idea with the Wildgoose, a tiny extending living unit which actually used a BMC 850 cc Mini-van chassis. But this later type adapted a slightly more powerful range of vehicles, notably the Bedford 8 cwt 1200 cc van, and the Ford Escort 1100 cc estate car. Unlike the Mini, their existing bodywork was capacious enough, and the addition of an elevating roof would accommodate all that is specified in Customs requirements. The living quarters were inevitably more confined than those of the larger conversions, but these vans could offer an unparalleled manoeuvrability and lightness of handling.

Martin Walter gave its smaller conversions not only the famous pram-hood extending roof, but also a pram-hood extending rear, to increase the length of the van when stationary. In view of their long-standing loyalty to Vauxhall, it is not surprising that their Roma, introduced in 1967, was based on the Bedford 8 cwt delivery van.

Torcars, a converter who went into business at Torrington, North Devon, in 1968, chose BLMC's equivalent model, the 1622 cc half-ton. One of their versions could sleep up to three

The ingenious little Wildgoose of the early 60s was based on an extended chassis of the 850 cc BMC Mini van. It was a coachbuilt model in that it substituted its own bodywork. It was an elevating-roof model in that its interior could be raised to standing height by a vertical extension. More important still, it was the first of the CDVs, or miniature motor caravans.

people. This model was slightly larger than the Roma, and required no extension at the rear. Since 1972 it has been trans-ferred to the newly-introduced Marina estate.

An excellent van, which offered itself to conversions of this kind, was the Ford Escort, with its racy but economic 1100 cc, or 1300 cc engine. Its potentialities tempted Martin Walter to stray from Bedford and to launch the Elba in 1968. The same basic van was used by Canterbury (once the firm linked with Peter Pitt) in their three-berth Siesta.

We have noticed earlier that the adoption of any particular vehicle as a basis for motor caravans depends in part on the interest shown in conversions by the motor manufacturer concerned. Lack of such interest is one reason why relatively few conversions made use of BMC's reasonably priced and eminently reliable 250 JU and J4. But much depends, too, on the timing of the cycle whereby, every fifteen years or so, the great companies re-tool their plants to bring out a whole new range of commercial vehicles. The Commer arrived on the scene late in 1959, at the very moment when the idea of motor caravanning was catching on. In the later 60s it was Ford's turn to bring out its new generation of models; and the Escort offered just the combination of extra roominess and extra performance for which the creators of mini-motor caravans were looking.

But far more important for the industry than the Escort was the Transit, launched simultaneously by Ford of England and Ford of Germany. For the first time a commercial van of no more than 2 litres could offer comfortable living quarters as it stood, without having its bodywork torn about. Like the Commer, it could take transverse beds, and soon all the major manufacturers were offering Transit conversions.

One motor manufacturer, while only too anxious to promote its products as motor caravans, adopted a quaintly restrictive attitude. This was Volkswagen, who for a long time refused to extend their guarantee to all conversions not carried out by one of their three authorized firms. They still refuse to sanction the fixing of the spare wheel on a bracket in front of the Kombi or Microbus – an almost essential practice in view of the limited interior space. Perhaps because of the challenge offered, it attracted the skill of the late J. P. White in the early 60s. His Devon Caravette was an example of all that an ingenious, well-tailored conversion should be, and his firm, not surprisingly, is now an integral part of Volkswagen (UK) Ltd.

Volkswagen's appeal lay in its reliability and economy (which some users claim are no greater than those of roomier, cheaper British vans), and in its unparalleled repair and spare-parts service throughout the globe. VW conversions might have become even more common in Britain had not sterling's devaluation in 1967 and 'float' in 1972 combined with a succession of Deutschemark revaluations to lift their price beyond the average motor caravanner's reach.

In Germany the Volkswagen has proved so popular with overseas visitors to Europe that special ships now ferry VW 'campers' across the Atlantic at bargain tariffs. A young American, John Wilkes, has even written an entertaining guide, *How to buy a used Volkswagen in Europe, keep it alive, and bring it home,* (dedicating it, amongst others, to Governor Ronald Reagan, an involuntary sponsor of its publication in 1973 at Berkeley University). There have also been some very fine conversions of the Mercedes diesel vans, though not on a mass-produced scale.

The only currency which dropped almost as rapidly as the pound during the late 60s and early 70s was the Italian lira. This was one reason for the growing popularity of the 903 cc Fiat in the early 70s. The economy of its light, low-compression engine was another advantage, and this model could be converted into a genuine mini motor caravan, with all the traditional features on a smaller, more manoeuvrable chassis.

The French, the most sophisticated campers of Europe, have made an unusual contribution. One of their light vans, the Renault Estafette 800 cc or 1000 cc is ideal for conversion, and has often received individual, do-it-yourself treatment. One of the better-known French trailer caravan manufacturers, Star of St-Brieuc, saw possibilities, and chose to offer, not a complete conversion, but instead a removable *aménagement* of furniture and fittings. This did not only cost a fraction of a complete motor caravan; it also left the Estafette free for other uses. Thus the *boucher* or *boulanger*, after delivering meat or bread all week, could slip his *aménagement* into place in ten minutes, and set off for the weekend in what Star called the *Studio-Car*. Later they introduced a similar *aménagement* for the Peugeot J7.

Since 1972 the Société Holiday, near Paris, has been producing coachbuilt *autocaravanes* on a number of chassis: Renault Estafette, Peugeot J7, Saviem SG2, and Citroën HV. Outwardly they look a little unwieldy beside comparable British models. But their interiors are of the same high standards as those of French trailer caravans, and they all have more emphasis placed on culinary fixtures rather than sanitary ones.

Finally, in 1972 CI Autohomes, Dormobile (as Martin Walter has been renamed since 1969), and Danbury, an Essex firm which had first made its name with VWs, all introduced conversions of the Japanese Toyota.

The first American products – which still form the majority of their recreational vehicles, or RecVs as they call motor caravans – were detachable 'piggy-back' caravans bolted on to the backs of pick-up vans. The advantage of these 'campers' was that, like the trailer caravan, they did not have to be renewed with the car, but could be transferred to the new pick-up. However, they are generally built of solid steel, and consequently are often criticized for being unnecessarily heavy.

CI Autohomes' elevating-roof 'Camper' conversion of the Toyota Hiace.

Many people found that the outsize US 'motorhomes' of the later 60s (afterwards imported by Wilsons) were too big and heavy to be driven with reasonable comfort. They do provide comfort on site; many now even feature a thermo waste-disposal system. But I have met Americans touring Europe who have praised the lightness and manoeuvrability of their hired British coachbuilt vans in comparison with their native products. No doubt this accounted for the great success of the Sunbeam Funwagon.

The most recent innovations in Britain reflect two of the overseas developments. First, Jones of Littlebourne, and then Walkers of Watford with their Suntrekker, have brought out British 'piggy-back' campers. Richard Holdsworth Conversions, having graduated from converting individual clients' vans to producing their own motor caravans, are now marketing the kits for the do-it-yourself enthusiast to install his own conversion.

This account of the history and development of motor caravans takes us to the last quarter of the twentieth century. But what of the future?

Two events of 1973 might seem at first sight to have called a halt to further progress. The first was the introduction of Value Added Tax in the UK, whereby all motor vehicles became liable for purchase tax, from which motor caravans, as utility vehicles, had previously been exempt. Motor caravans no longer have a $22\frac{1}{2}\%$ cost advantage over the private car. The second, of course, was the dramatic rise in petrol prices at the end of the year. In addition, there were price increases throughout the motor industry during the course of 1974. In 1975 prices continued their upward spiral, and the imposition of Car Tax in addition to VAT eliminated any cost advantage the motor caravan may once have possessed.

But the prices of alternative purchases have risen more steeply still. Hotels are fast becoming beyond the reach of anyone not on an expense account. That celebration of retirement, the world cruise, now costs thousands of pounds rather than hundreds. Even the package tour has been loaded with currency adjustments and fuel surcharges, or even placed in jeopardy by agents' bankruptcies. In relation to these increases the motor caravan is no more expensive than it has ever been.

At the same time there has been a growing awareness of what the motor caravan has to offer. It is now commonplace to see Highwaymen parked in suburban driveways, Dormobiles standing in city streets, or Auto-Sleepers alongside at the traffic lights. Forward-looking travel journalists have realized its potentialities, and Nigel Buxton has devoted some fine writing to motor caravanning in the *Sunday Telegraph*.

The questions that are put to an owner today are altogether better informed than ten years ago. Inquirers already know what a motor caravan is, and are only anxious to fill in details of performance and layout. An increasing number of people are gradually coming to realize that with no greater expenditure of fuel than they would use on routine driving at home they could see the world – and that there is probably no other way that they ever are going to see it.

What vans will they choose? I believe that they will continue to buy coachbuilt vans, commercial conversions, and self-converted vans. But for reasons both of economy and flexibility, however, I believe that we will see more of those two relative newcomers: the mini motor caravan, and the 'piggy-back' camper.

Appendix: Complete list of motor caravans in production

Readers contemplating a conversion, whether by themselves or a professional, will want to know its engine capacity (to give them some indication of its power and consumption), its overall length (to know how much it will cost on ferries), and the dimensions of its 'useful' area behind the cab (to know what they can fit in and how). They may also be interested not only in models in current production, but in those still readily available on the second-hand market. In the list below no allowance is made in the 'useful area' for wheel arches, sloping sides, domed roofs, or, in the case of the Fiat and Volkswagen, for their space-stealing rear engines.

Current models

Bedford SWB and LWB (1759 cc and 2279 cc)
Overall length: SWB 167.8 in, 4.26 m
　　　　　　　　LWB 187.8 in, 4.77 m
useful area: SWB 100 in, 2.54 m long
　　　　　　　　75.7 in, 1.92 m wide
　　　　　　　　54.4 in, 1.38 m high
　　　　　　　LWB 119 in, 3.03 m long
　　　　　　　　75.7 in, 1.92 m wide
　　　　　　　　60.6 in, 1.53 m high

Bedford Leyland 240 (1622 cc and 1798 cc)
overall length: 182 in, 4.62 m
useful area: 97.8 in, 2.49 m long
　　　　　　　64.5 in, 1.64 m wide
　　　　　　　53.5 in, 1.36 m high

British Leyland 7 cwt and 10 cwt (1098 cc and 1275 cc)
overall length: 165.5 in, 4.21 m
useful area: 72 in, 1.85 m long
　　　　　　　57.5 in, 1.46 m wide
　　　　　　　39 in, 1 m high

Commer 1500 and 2500 (1720 cc and 1750 cc)
overall length: 167.8 in, 4.26 m
useful area: 105 in, 2.66 m long
　　　　　　　70.5 in, 1.79 m wide
　　　　　　　54.8 in, 1.39 m high

Fiat 850 (903 cc)
overall length: 147 in, 3.73 m
useful area: 84 in, 2.13 m long
　　　　　　　50 in, 1.25 m wide
　　　　　　　46 in, 1.18 m high (high-top version 54 in, 1.38 m)

Ford Transit (1663 cc and 1996 cc)
overall length: 175 in, 4.44 m
useful area: 90 in, 2.29 m long
　　　　　　　72 in, 1.83 m wide
　　　　　　　SWB 53.5 in, 1.36 m high
　　　　　　　LWB 59.5 in, 1.51 m high

Ford Escort (1098 cc, 1298 cc and 1600 cc)
overall length: 162 in, 4.11 m
useful area: 72 in, 1.83 m long
　　　　　　　61 in, 1.55 m wide
　　　　　　　38 in, 0.96 m high

Land Rover (2286 cc and 2625 cc)
overall length: LWB 175 in, 4.44 m
useful area: 72.7 in, 1.85 m long
　　　　　　　56.8 in, 1.44 m wide
　　　　　　　52 in, 1.32 m high

Mercedes (2197 cc)
overall length: 205 in, 5.20 m
useful area: 132 in, 3.35 m long
　　　　　　　66 in, 1.68 m wide
　　　　　　　73.5 in, 1.87 m high

Toyota Hiace (1587 cc)
overall length: 170 in, 4.31 m
useful area: 103 in, 2.63 m long
                59 in, 1.50 m wide
                52 in, 1.32 m high

Volkswagen (1600 cc and 2000 cc)
overall length: 178 in, 4.50 m
useful area: 110 in, 2.80 m long
                59 in, 1.50 m wide
                55.1 in, 1.40 m high

Models no longer in production
Bedford CAS and CAL (1494 cc and 1598 cc)
overall length: CAS 162 in, 4.11 m
                CAL 174 in, 4.41 m
useful area: CAS 90 in, 2.28 m long
                CAL 100 in, 2.54 m long
                72 in, 1.82 m wide
                53 in, 1.35 m high

BMC JU 250 (1622 cc)
overall length: 174.5 in, 4.43 m
useful area: 108 in, 2.72 m long
                67 in, 1.70 m wide
                57.5 in, 1.45 m high

BMC J2 (1489 cc and 1622 cc)
overall length: 168 in, 4.27 m
useful area: 108 in, 2.72 m long
                69 in, 1.75 m wide
                55 in, 1.40 m high

BLMC J4 (1489 cc and 1622 cc)
overall length: 159 in, 4.04 m
useful area: 95 in, 2.41 m long
                60 in, 1.52 m wide
                52.5 in, 1.34 m high